SCOTTISH
EXECUTIONS
ASSASSINATIONS
AND
MURDERS

Martin Horan

D1462243

Chambers

CHAMBERS
An imprint of Larousse plc
43–45 Annandale Street
Edinburgh EH7 4AZ

First published by Chambers 1990
Reprinted 1994

A CIP catalogue record for this book is
available from the British Library

ISBN 0 550 20056 8

Illustrations by Julie Horan
© Larousse plc
Cover design by John Marshall

Typeset by Bookworm Typesetting Ltd, Edinburgh
Printed in Singapore by
Singapore National Printers Ltd

Contents

Preface

Scotland's turbulent history evokes images of war, treachery, blood-letting, assassination and murder. And no small wonder. Few nations have had so many monarchs murdered throughout the course of their history as have the Scots. Indeed, few nations have had as many *murderers* among their monarchs.

Long before the Scots first arrived from Ireland carnage was a way of life with the native Britons and Picts. Such was their ferocity that even the mighty Roman Empire was unable to subdue them and was forced simply to build a wall to keep them out. This tradition of violence continued through the centuries: monarchs and nobles gained power through murdering those who had it. So assassination and murder is nothing new in the annals of Scottish history.

This small book deals with a cross-section of terrible deaths of some of Scotland's residents throughout the ages, monarch and commoner alike. Not all are strictly historical executions, assassinations and murders — though most of them happen to be so — because I intended to include those sad ends that I personally thought would be most interesting reading, but a line had to be drawn! A history of Scottish executions, assassinations and murders from any *week* in its gory past, up to the '45 rebellion, would fill tomes.

Although the definition of 'execution' is fairly clear, the distinction between an assassination and a murder is not (after all, assassination is murder). The definition I have used is that the victim of an assassination is generally a figure in authority and that the crime is committed for political gain.

Despite the 'proud history of Scottish mayhem', other nations possess histories as bloody and have lived under tyrants just as blood-thirsty. But, not having that Celtic preoccupation with things gory, they would rather forget them. The Scots, on the contrary, would prefer to record them for posterity.

This book is, in a sense, an introduction to and a small reminder of Scotland's gory past.

SCOTTISH EXECUTIONS . . .

The Execution of Wallace
William Wallace

Scotland's greatest hero died an ignominious death. His execution, which took place in London was barbaric beyond measure. In a way it was a fitting end to his tragic life: he was often betrayed in life and it was through betrayal he died on 22 August 1305.

Wallace, a giant of a man, actually allowed himself to be taken. His capture happened at Robroystoun near Glasgow where he trusted a traitor named Menteith who promised him protection if he would permit himself to be bound and brought before the authorities. According to Menteith, the authorities in Scotland merely required Wallace's word that he would not war with them. However, as soon as Wallace was bound and tied, he was dispatched to England to face the 'justice' of the tyrant Edward I.

He was tried at Westminster for treason. A catalogue of his alleged crimes was read out to him. Each 'crime' brought a chorus of jeers and hoots of anger from the audience of whom not one would have dared to insult Wallace but for the chains and ropes which bound him. When he asked for a defence lawyer he was shouted down. He then denounced his trial as a farce and refused to say another word. However, he broke his vowed silence when he was accused of treason against the King: 'I have never betrayed Edward, nor an English lord, for I never submitted to them. You cannot break a word you never gave, and my allegiance is and always has been to the legitimate King of Scots and to Scotland. Edward is a tyrant, usurper and a criminal fit for the rope.' So saying, he spat on the floor to show his disgust. That only drove the English lords to further indignant rage, which Wallace's indifference could hardly appease.

When the hubbub died down the atrocious sentence was read out slowly and deliberately. The intended effect failed. Wallace did not bat an eyelid, despite the false allegations against him. For instance, he was accused of murdering innocent women and children. This must have been the more galling to Wallace as he

3

himself had witnessed English soldiers preparing to burn a woman alive.

Seeing Wallace and his greatly outnumbered group in the distance, some English soldiers built a large fire on which to throw the wife of a Scottish patriot. They were ordered to do so by a Scottish knight named Butler who hoped by this savagery to lay a trap for Wallace and avenge his father and grandfather (both of whom had been slain by Wallace for their treason against Scotland).

Wallace, unable to stand by and watch the atrocity without intervening, broke from his stronghold shouting, 'You repulsive English cowards, do you make war on women? You should be ashamed of yourselves. Here I am; come and get me if *you* are not too woman-ish to try.'

And now *he* was being accused of the very thing he despised.

When the farce of a trial was over, he was dragged outside to the jeers of the crowd. He was strapped, naked, to a gate pulled by horses; he was strapped head downwards in such a way that his head would bump against the ground when the horses moved off.

From Westminster he was dragged to Smithfield. At that time Smithfield was a country village; now it is in the centre of London. No-one knows the exact spot where Wallace was executed, but it is reckoned to be some-where in Cowcross Street, a back street which runs between Farringdon Street and St John Street. The only building in Smithfield which actually stood at that time and is still standing is the church of St Bartholomew. It was probably the last building Wallace's dying eyes saw.

Any ordinary mortal would not have even reached Smithfield alive had he suffered the same torturous ordeal. Smithfield is a good two miles at least from Westminster, and Wallace was not dragged there directly, as one contemporary chronicler has shown (the words are rendered into modern English spelling):

> And when the judges had pronounced the Decree the soldiers took Wallace from Westminster Hall, and did bind him with stout cords, whereto were harnessed four horses. And thus they dragged him by the banks of the Thames River to the Tower, followed by a great multitude who jeered at him. And when they came

4

to the Tower they turned the horses northwards past the convent of the poor Clares, by the way called the Minories, and thus by Aldgate to the Elms, which was the place appointed for execution. And all this was done there as had been decreed and ordained by the Judges to the honour of Our Lord the King, and to the effrayment of all rebellious and sacrilegious subjects.

It is astonishing to think that Wallace was dragged all that distance and still remained alive. Not only was his head bumped along the ground, he was also pelted with sticks, stones and rubbish by the enraged crowd. Today we may well ask what could have possessed the people to have behaved so cruelly. However, if we bear in mind the lies they had been told about Wallace, on top of his legendary guerrilla warfare, their behaviour does not seem quite so barbaric. There was a well-known story about him at that time – recorded in the *Lanercost Chronicle* – which claimed that when the brave but rash de Cressingham was killed at the Battle of Stirling Bridge, Wallace had his skin flayed and made into a baldrick for his sword. Other reports stated it was cut into saddle girths for the Scots cavalry or that pieces were sent throughout Scotland to declare victory.

5

By the time Wallace reached West Smithfield he was nearly unconscious. (Ironically, Smithfield is now a meat market where animals' carcasses hang in abundance and Londoners pass through the district blissfully unaware of the other kind of butchery that happened there over 680 years ago.) He passed out several times and it was nothing short of miraculous that he regained consciousness when he reached the scaffold. Even so, he still inspired fear among his captors: when they unbound him they kept his hands tied well behind his back.

When he was helped to his feet he shouted for a priest to confess his sins. According to the Scottish poet, Blind Harry, Edward forbade this. Wallace then cried out for the psalter he always carried – or any psalter that might be available – to be held before his eyes. When Edward, who sat among the nobles in a stand built for the occasion, was about to forbid this too, the Archbishop of Canterbury intervened. Edward threatened to have him arrested if he dared listen to the condemned man's confession but the Archbishop retorted that he would have the despot excommunicated if he did. The Archbishop then listened to Wallace's confession – or at least to as much of it as he could utter – and a priest came forward with a psalter. This done, the swaying Wallace was helped up to the scaffold to face a severe, black-masked, bare-armed executioner almost as huge as himself. The rope was fixed around Wallace's neck and pulled until he was well off the platform. He was left thus, hanging from the gibbet, twitching and writhing, for about two minutes. The rope was then released and Wallace dropped down on to the scaffold, unconscious but still alive.

The executioner then unsheathed a sharp knife and castrated Wallace, throwing his genitals into a burning brazier. He then slashed open his belly, stuck his hands into the enormous wound and pulled out the entrails. These were also thrown into the fire. It has been said that Wallace was still alive at that point.

Next, the heart was hacked out of the breast and held aloft to the crowd who roared their appreciation.

That barbaric act was followed by another. This time the executioner swapped his knife for an axe and continued his butchery by chopping off the arms, the legs, and finally the head. The great head was also held up to the cheering crowd. Thus, the man who was called 'the saviour of Scotland' and 'the secular saint' met his terrible end. Thus, Smithfield gained the title of 'the Calvary of Scottish Independence'.

His head was hung from Tower Bridge and the limbs were sent to Newcastle, Berwick, Stirling and Perth where they were hung from public buildings to serve as a warning to other 'rebels'.

Statues, plaques and other monuments are dotted all over Scotland showing the esteem and affection with which Scots have held Wallace since that fateful August day.

A Martyr of Faith

Patrick Hamilton

Before James V came of age, the Reformation had made considerable progress in Scotland. Many merchants and seamen had already brought bibles and Lutheran works into the country, and although the Church forbade the influx of 'all such filth' the prohibition seemed only to stimulate further interest.

As a youth, Patrick Hamilton must have read much of this literature because he was inspired to go to Wittenberg to make Luther's acquaintance. After being instructed there in theology, he was advised by Luther himself to return to Scotland to preach the principles of the Reformation to his fellow countrymen.

When he returned to Scotland his sermons had such a profound effect on the populace that the clergy became alarmed. In 1528, they decoyed Hamilton to St Andrews where he was seized and condemned to be burned alive.

A stake was set in front of the old college of St Andrews. Before he was tied to it, he was offered his life if he would cast a burning faggot on to the others as a sign that he recanted. He refused.

As soon as he was bound to the stake he prayed for God's mercy on his prosecutors and implored strength to endure his pains. Fire was set on the pile, but it was slow in igniting. Gunpowder was placed among the wood. It exploded, scorching Hamilton's left hand and the side of his face. The wood was too damp for a quick blaze and he roasted slowly and choked with the fumes. He cried to his executors to throw more gunpowder on to the wood.

As additional fuel was applied, the friars moved around the pyre jeering, 'Convert heretic! Call upon our Lady and say, "Hail, Queen of Heaven".' He replied calmly: 'You are late with your advice. If I had chosen to recant I need not have been here.'

More fuel was brought and a baker, perhaps out of pity and in the hope of hastening Hamilton's end, threw a bale of straw on to the fire. A blast of wind raised the flames dramatically 'and a fitful gust threw them aside in a jet so sudden and fierce' that the front of a monk's cowl was burnt completely.

Hamilton's soft voice could still be heard through the roaring of the flames as he committed his mother to the hospitality of some friends. His last words were, 'How long, Lord, shall darkness overwhelm this kingdom? How long wilt thou suffer this tyranny of men? Lord Jesus receive my spirit.' The chain binding him to the stake had become red-hot and burned deeply into his stomach and sides. Seeing this, a spectator cried out for a sign of his constancy to his beliefs. He replied by raising three fingers of his half-consumed hand. He held them in that position, steadily, until he ceased to live.

The clergy thought they had silenced him forever but the awestruck crowd, hearing only the roar of the flames over the dead man's bones, were given something to think about. The burning of Hamilton actually helped the Reformation. Protestantism got such a strong hold in Scotland that a gentleman said to the Bishop of St Andrews, 'My lord, if ye will burn any mair, let them be burned in cellars for the reek o' Patrick Hamilton has affected as many as it blew upon.'

Queen Beheaded

Mary Queen of Scots

Mary Queen of Scots' motto was 'My end is my beginning' – which is apt because she is best known for her execution. Although she was involved in countless dramas, schemes and scandals throughout her life, most people remember her as the Queen who was beheaded on the orders of her cousin, Queen Elizabeth I of England.

With the aid of the Earl Bothwell, whom she subsequently married, Mary murdered her husband, Lord Darnley. The common people of Scotland accused her of this in vain until her letters to Bothwell – now known as the 'casket letters' – fell into the hands of the Earl Morton. These letters showed her to be an accomplice in the murder of Lord Darnley. Those who wish to believe in her innocence now maintain that they are forgeries, but no-one made this claim at the time, not even Mary's partisans either in parliament or elsewhere.

The 'privy-council and nobility' charged Bothwell with the murder of Darnley on 12 June 1567. Three days later, backed by about 4000 men, he tried to fight the government troops. Defeated, he rode off, never to see Mary again. The Queen surrendered.

On 24 July 1567, Mary signed three documents. The first renounced her crown in favour of her son, the second appointed Moray as Regent and the third named several lords as a collective regency until Moray returned to Scotland.

The English Queen was angry and disappointed. She believed that, as her subjects, the Scottish lords had no right to judge Mary and she refused to recognise the new government. However, her ambassador reported that the Scottish people firmly believed that Mary was guilty of Darnley's murder and wanted her to stand trial, and that the sympathy of the Scottish council lay with the people.

It was thought that Mary would be secure in Loch Leven Castle – built on a small island in the middle of the loch – but on the night of 2 May 1558 18-year-old

William Douglas got hold of the castle keys, sneaked the Queen through the gates and rowed her to the shore where Lord Seton and other friends were waiting. Eleven days later, her supporters were defeated at the Battle of Langside and she fled to England for protection.

Her escape to England put Elizabeth in a difficult position, as English Catholics, who were numerous and powerful, saw Mary as their legitimate Queen and her presence in the country made insurrection more likely. However, if Elizabeth allowed Mary to leave England, she would certainly go to France for assistance to subdue her subjects and regain her kingdom.

Elizabeth sent her messengers to Mary, who was living safely in Carlisle where she 'recovered her spirits, and resumed her intrigues'. They expressed the Queen's sympathies and stated the only terms on which Elizabeth would aid her. First she had to be cleared of any involvement in her husband's murder. Elizabeth became arbiter between Mary and her subjects.

A conference was called at York. The Earl of Moray attended, bringing the casket letters with him. It was with great reluctance that he produced them, but he had no alternative. The English commissioners compared the letters to Mary's other writings and concluded they were the same. None had a shadow of a doubt – not even the Duke of Norfolk, whose later intrigues and marriage scheme with Mary sent him to the block.

Mary tried to have the Regent, the Earl of Moray, intercepted and murdered at Northallerton and the casket letters destroyed. Moray heard of the plot and avoided the trap. He was murdered on his return to Edinburgh by James Hamilton of Bothwellhaugh who shot him from a window in the house of Archbishop Hamilton. The bullet passed through the Regent's body and also killed a horse. Bothwellhaugh received a pension soon after from Mary's jointure as Queen-dowager of France.

She was seldom without a plot or intrigue at hand and kept up correspondence with the Guises, the King of Spain and the Pope. She was in alliance with all of Elizabeth's disaffected subjects and encouraged several plots against the Queen's life. The death of Elizabeth would make her the Queen of England. 'The wonder,' as one Scots historian put it, 'is not that Elizabeth brought Mary to the scaffold at last, but that she refrained so long.'

Mary was held in different places during her 15 years of captivity: Carlisle, Bolton, Tutbury, Sheffield, Wingfield, Chatsworth, Chartley, Tixall and eventually Coventry. Though she complained often of her captivity, she still lived like a Queen. She had 16 horses and frequently rode out hunting; she had all the privileges and amusements of a Queen and was so well treated by the Earl of Shrewsbury that his countess became jealous and quarrelled furiously with the captive Mary.

It had been arranged between the two Queens that if Mary was acquitted of her part in Darnley's murder Elizabeth would reinstate her with full powers, although she might have to rule with her son. But Mary was brought to trial for another plot. She had planned to assassinate Elizabeth, aid and abet a Spanish invasion and incite a Catholic rebellion both in England and Scotland. She was condemned by a letter in her hand.

Still Elizabeth did not want to sentence Mary to death, although she knew that as long as Mary lived her own life would never be safe from the Jesuits who, eager for a Catholic monarch, 'would dog her life with dagger and poison'.

Mary was sentenced to death on 25 October 1586, when the commissioners met in the Star Chamber at Westminster. A few days later the English parliament confirmed the sentence and petitioned the reluctant Elizabeth for its sanction. The parliament urged that if she had no regard for her own life she did have duties to the throne, the freedom of England and the safety of the nation's religion.

On 8 February 1587, the Queen of Scots was taken to the castle hall of Fotheringay to be executed. She arrived to find the hall filled with about 300 spectators. Both scaffold and block were draped in black cloth and, but for a long, white veil trailing to the floor, Mary herself was dressed in black down to her Spanish leather shoes.

People prayed loudly. There was a competition of Latin prayers against English ones but, in spite of the excitement, Mary remained calm and even cheerful. She seemed quite indifferent to her impending fate and actually joked in mock complaint, when her two ladies – Jane Kennedy and Elizabeth Curle – held her outer garments, that never before had she been forced to disrobe before such company. She said it to calm *them* because they were so nervous and distraught, but they wept in spite of the well-meaning jest and Mary scolded them.

Then, with the help of her ladies, the executioner and his assistant aided the Queen in undressing. The official recorder noted that she undressed so quickly 'that it seemed as she was in haste to be gone out of the world'. Her underclothing was red and one of her ladies gave her a pair of red sleeves, the colour of blood. This was the liturgical colour of martyrdom in the Roman Catholic Church.

The axeman and his assistant knelt before her and begged forgiveness for their part in her execution. This was customary and almost a formality with executioners. She replied, 'I forgive you with all my heart for now I hope you shall make an end of all my troubles.' She prayed that her enemies be forgiven and asked the saints to make intercession for her.

Jane Kennedy tied a blindfold round her head. It was a white cloth embroidered with gold that Mary had herself chosen the previous night. It also held her hair in place that her neck would be bared for the axe. She knelt and groped for the block, placing her head on it. As she did so, she recited a psalm in Latin. Then the axeman removed her hands, with which she was steadying her chin, for they were in the direct line of the axe. So she stretched out her arms and cried out: '*In manus tuas, Domine, confide spiritum meum.*' She shouted it three or four times.

The executioner's assistant put his hand on Mary to steady her for the blow. But, as it fell, the first blow missed the neck and cut into the back of the head. Mary's lips moved and someone nearby thought she uttered 'Sweet Jesus'. The second blow all but severed the head. A piece of skin or sinew held it to the body. It was severed by the executioner using his axe as a saw.

He then held up the head to the spectators and cried out, 'God save the Queen!' The lips on the severed head still moved and continued to do so till quarter of an hour after the fatal blow. What the axeman did not know was that Mary went to the block wearing a wig. As he held the head aloft it fell from the wig to the floor. The stunned spectators remained silent. The silence was broken when the Dean of Peterborough called out, 'So perish all the Queen's enemies.'

Without the auburn wig, the crowd saw the head had close-cropped grey hair. The face was so changed by death that it could not be recognised as Mary's.

When the executioner bent to take the dead Queen's garters he found her lapdog, a Skye terrier, had hidden under her skirts. It could not be coaxed away and it ran to the bleeding neck. It became so covered with blood that it had to be washed repeatedly. The dog refused to eat afterwards and eventually pined to death.

The blood-stained block was burned, as were Mary's clothes and other belongings so they would not be made into relics. In the late afternoon the body was stripped and certain organs, including the heart, were removed and buried secretly – the exact spot has never been revealed – for the same reason. The body was then wrapped in a wax shroud and locked up in a lead coffin. It was given no burial but was walled up in Fotheringay Castle until Sunday 30 July of the same year when it received a proper burial, with full royal pomp, in Peterborough Cathedral. There it remained until 1612 when Mary's son, James VI of Scotland and I of England, had it removed to Westminster where it now lies under a tomb of great splendour.

Morton's Ironical End

The Regent Morton

It is understandable why the Regent Morton introduced the 'Maiden' – Scotland's version of the French guillotine – into the country. There is a belief that desperate situations require desperate remedies and during the reign of Mary Queen of Scots and the minority of her son, James VI, Scotland was in a desperate situation.

Violent lawlessness was rife. Ambushes and murders by the lords and their men occurred daily. One day two earls and their retainers were going in opposite directions in a narrow Stirling lane. Because the last two men jostled each other, pistols and swords were instantly drawn. When the fighting died down, most men on both sides were seriously injured and one of the earls lay dead.

There was a similar clash between two lords outside Parliament House in Edinburgh. When the magistrates arrived they threatened to open fire on both sides if they did not stop fighting – but dozens were already injured and one man lay dead.

The lords were vicious and unruly and no jury would dare convict them. Whenever they were summoned to the courts to answer for their crimes they brought their armies with them to intimidate the accusers. No wonder Thomas Carlyle, the Scottish historian, called the lords 'a selfish, ferocious, unprincipled set of hyenas'. In those days the greed for power was so great that heiresses were kidnapped and forced to marry against their wills. Even the Regent Moray stole Queen Mary's jewels and sold them to Queen Elizabeth.

So it is hardly surprising that when Morton became Regent he wanted stringent measures against lawlessness. He knew just how unscrupulous the Scottish lords could be because he himself was unscrupulous. He had amassed a fortune from bribes, fines and the forfeiture of his opponents' lands. It was well-known that the best insurance against losing a lawsuit was to leave a bag of gold on his table.

Morton agreed to pardon the Laird of Innes of a murder charge in return for his estate. The Laird was foolish

15

enough to get drunk and boast that he would like to see Morton *try* to take his lands. The following day Innes was beheaded and his lands became Morton's.

The King did not like the stout Regent, partly because he was the most powerful noble in Scotland from the most powerful house of Douglas and partly because he had contempt for the arts, of which the King was a fervent patron. Consequently, James was pleased when Captain James Stewart entered the council and fell on his knees before the young King, accusing Morton of being involved in the murder of Darnley, the King's father.

The trial was a farce; almost every man on the jury was a sworn enemy. They condemned him to be 'headed, quartered and drawn' the next day. When he was offered the choice of being hanged or 'headed' he replied that it was a matter of indifference to him. So they stuck to the sentence.

He went back to his cell and dined heartily. After his meal, he wrote a long letter to the King. When James, a boy approaching his 15th birthday, received Morton's letter, he heartlessly refused to read it. Instead, the young King paced the room, snapping his fingers.

When the ministers of Edinburgh attended the doomed man to prepare him for death, he openly declared all that he knew about Darnley's murder. Bothwell, he said, strove hard to get him involved in the assassination but he refused. When he was reminded that he was guilty of concealing the plot, he replied: 'To whom could I hae revealed it? To the Queen? She was the doer of it. To Darnley? I durst nae for my life; for I kenned him to be such a bairn that there was naething telt him he wad reveal it to her again. And therefore I durst in nae way reveal it.'

At about four o'clock in the afternoon he was led out to the scaffold erected at the Mercat Cross. On mounting it he was bidden to stand at each of its four corners and address the crowd each time. 'His countenance, his voice, and manner, were as calm and dignified as when he ruled Scotland'. There was no shortage of his enemies among the spectators: the Laird of Ferniehirst 'dressed out with large ruffs' stood at a window opposite the scaffold enjoying the spectacle. Lord Seton, one of the jurors who tried him, stood on steps at a building entrance nearby with his two sons to glory in the execution.

Morton put his head on the block of the 'Maiden' and still remained calm. One can only wonder what his thoughts were, for not only did he introduce the gruesome machine into Scotland but he had it built to the design he liked best, based on one he had seen at Halifax in Yorkshire. Now he was going to die on it. He kept repeating 'Lord Jesus receive my soul' until the blade fell.

The head was set on an iron spike on the highest part of the tolbooth gable facing the main street. It remained there for 18 months until the King gave permission for it to be taken down. It was put in a fine cloth and carried, reverently, to the resting place of the body in Greyfriars' Cemetery where it was buried. 'The Laird of Carmichael carried it, shedding tears abundantly by the way.'

Bravery Despite Betrayal
The Marquis of Montrose

James Graham, the Marquis of Montrose, remained calm and dignified when he was handed over to his enemies by the betrayal of a friend – by no means a rare occurrence in Scotland's history. Even when his captors, the Scottish Parliament, denied him any object or instrument 'lest he should have done harm to himself' he remained aloof, commentating disdainfully to his gaoler: 'You need not be at so much pains. Before I was taken I had a prospect of this cruel treatment and, if my conscience would have allowed me, I could have dispatched myself.'

Many an historical Scottish worthy went to the block, the 'Maiden' or the rope, with a similar indifference to their fate. How often was it true stoical acceptance of their end and how often was it pure Scottish stubbornness, refusing to the last to give their enemies the satisfaction of their fear?

Montrose's gaolers later admitted that he remained calm throughout the morning before he received his sentence. Considering he had scarcely slept an hour since he was first incarcerated the previous night this was no mean feat. He had also been refused the service of a barber when he asked for one. Between 10 a.m. and midday he was taken to the bar to receive his sentence. He still kept his wits when he was told that he was to be hanged, drawn and quartered. His head was to remain in Edinburgh and his other parts sent to Glasgow, Dundee, Aberdeen, etc. After listening patiently to the sentence, he delivered a long, eloquent speech in his defence.

Sir James Balfour's notes on the proceedings in parliament that day state:

> The Lord Chancellor replied, punctually proving him, by acts of his hostility, to be a person most infamous, perjured, treacherous and, of all that this land ever brought forth, the most cruel and inhuman butcher and murderer of his nation, a sworn enemy to the Covenant and peace of his country and one whose boundless pride and ambition had lost the father, and

by his wicked counsels had done what in him lay to destroy the son likewise.

Montrose made no reply but knelt as he was ordered and received the sentence officially from his executioner. As soon as it was delivered he retorted that, 'according to our Scots proverb, "a messenger should neither be headed nor hanged".' Lord Loudon, president of the parliament, replied to Montrose, 'It is you and such as you that are a great snare to princes and draw them to give such bloody commissions.' He was then sent back to prison.

Because he was an excommunicant, no friend or relation was allowed to be with him. The Kirk, however, permitted three men to sit with him. At least one of these was a minister. They probably tried to get him to see things from the Covenanters' viewpoint, for Montrose is reported to have exclaimed, 'I pray you, gentlemen, let me die in peace.'

One of the men, Robert Baillie, said he only spoke to Montrose of some things concerning his spiritual life, but the Wigton manuscript states:

> He was no sooner carried back to prison, than the ministers with fresh assaults invaded him, aggravating the terror of the sentence, in order to affright him. He said he was much beholden to the parliament for the honour they put on him; for, says he, 'I think it is a greater honour to have my head standing on the port of this town, for this quarrel, than to have my picture in the King's bed-chamber. I am beholden to you that, lest my loyalty should be forgotten, ye have appointed five of your most eminent towns to bear witness of it to posterity.'

The same chronicle attests to his presence of mind in the face of inescapable death:

> His friends were not suffered to come near him; and a guard was kept in the chamber beside him, so that he had no time or place for his private devotions, but in their hearing. Yet it is acknowledged by them all that he rested kindly those nights, except sometimes when at his prayers, as ever they themselves did.

Further proof of his presence of mind and indifference to his fate is the following poem which he composed on the eve of his execution:

19

Let them bestow on ev'ry Airth a Limb;
Open all my veins that I may swim
To Thee my Saviour, in that crimson lake;
Then place my par-boil'd head upon a Stake;
Scatter my Ashes, throw them in the Air:
Lord (since Thou know'st where all these Atoms are)
I'm hopeful, once Thou'lt recollect my Dust,
And confident thou'lt raise me with the Just.

Some romantics claim he was denied pen and paper and scored the poem on a window with a diamond in his ring.

Early the next morning, Tuesday 21 May 1650, Montrose asked the Captain of the Guard the reason for the fanfare of trumpets and drums outside. He was told it was to summon the citizens and soldiers to arms in case the Marquis' many supporters might try to free him. Montrose was amused. 'Do I, who have been such a terror to these worthies during my life, continue still so formidable to them now, when about to die? But let them look to themselves; for even after I am dead, I will be continually present to their wicked consciences, and become more dreadful to them than when in life.'

Soon afterwards one of the parliament, Sir Archibald Johnson, entered the cell. He sneered as he watched Montrose comb his hair and made an impertinent comment. The Graham answered with a smile. 'While my head is my own I will dress and adorn it. But when it becomes yours you may treat it as you please.'

He was taken to the centre of Edinburgh's Grassmarket where the gallows were made ready. They were the extraordinary height of 30 feet. Montrose had to walk to them and still no friend was allowed near to offer him comfort.

'To the bitter disappointment of his enemies, Montrose went through this trying scene with the magnanimity of a hero, the dignity of a nobleman, the grace and gallantry of a perfect gentleman, and the well-grounded hope of a true Christian.' In fact, Montrose tried to comfort the crowd, encouraging them not to be saddened by the outrage of his execution: 'Doth it not often happen to the righteous according to the ways of the wicked, and to the wicked according to the ways of the righteous? Doth not a just man perish in his righteousness and a wicked man prosper in his malice?'

Amid interruptions, he delivered an eloquent and lengthy speech. When he had finished he asked if he could keep his hat on but the request was refused. He then climbed the scaffold dressed 'in his red scarlet cassock, in a very stately manner, and never spoke a word'. But when the hangman put the noose over his head he asked, 'How long shall I hang there?' He was told three hours. He gave the hangman three or four pieces of gold and forgave him before asking him to push him as soon as he raised his hands. Weeping, the hangman did as he was bidden.

As Montrose was pushed the audience gave out a unanimous groan. Even some of his enemies wept. Lord Lorn, however, 'mocked and laughed in the midst of that weeping assembly, and staying afterwards to see him hewn in pieces, triumphed at every stroke which was bestowed upon his mangled body'.

On the orders of Lady Napier the mutilated trunk was later dug up from its mean grave and the heart taken from it and wrapped up in fine linen and brought to her. She had craftsmen encase it in an egg of steel made from the blade of Montrose's own sword. This was in turn encased in 'a rich box of gold'. It was sent to Montrose's eldest son, a refugee in Flanders, to go through as many amazing adventures as when it beat bravely in the hero's breast.

The Last Witch
Grissel Jaffrey

Every country in Europe has a history stained with the blood of innocent people executed as witches or warlocks. Scotland was far from being the exception. In fact, in Scotland witches were punished long before the great witch craze swept Europe in the 15th and 16th centuries. In AD 840, a law was passed ordering the tongue of any practitioner of magic to be cut out. Later, the punishment was to be death by 'wirrying' (strangulation) then the body was to burned at the stake.

One famous case was that of Lady Glamis. She was accused of attempting to assassinate James V by means of witchcraft. After a long trial she was taken on 7 July 1537, 'to the Castle Hill of Edinburgh, and there burnt in a fire as a traitor'.

James VI was a fervent believer in witchcraft. He wrote *Daemonologie*, a massive tome on the subject, and set about wiping out witches with gusto. During his reign, heinous tortures were inflicted on innocent people in order to extract a confession of witchcraft. The most common tortures were the 'pilniewinks' or thumbscrews, the 'cashielaws' (an iron case that fitted around the leg and was heated) and the 'boot'. The latter was made of iron and was tightened by the insertion of iron rods which crushed the foot and ankle as they were inserted. Another common torture was to 'thraw in the heid wi' rapes' – twisting knotted ropes around the head.

Once accused of witchcraft there was no way out. Confession under torture was proof of your guilt and refusal to confess was further proof. Once the inevitable proof was established, the victim went to the stake.

James VI himself witnessed a 'trial' during which one such accused had his nails torn out by pincers and his leg crushed so badly in the boot that 'the blood and marrow spurted forth'. Incredibly, the man still would not confess. James claimed that his refusal to confess was further proof that the devil had entered his heart. The man was subsequently burned at the stake.

Status was no protection against accusation, which

struck noblemen as well as commoner. Thousands of innocents perished as witches between James' reign and the burning of Janet Horne, the last witch in Scotland, in 1722. Much to the annoyance of the Presbytery an act was passed in 1735 by George II repealing all the statutes against witchcraft.

The Presbytery were active in encouraging witch-hunts all over Scotland, the cruellest times being during 1660 to 1685. There were many famous trials but one case, which was later covered up, was the 'Martyr-dom of Grissel Jaffrey', the last person to be burned for witchcraft in Dundee. There are no records of any 'witch' persecutions in the Dundee kirk annals, though they certainly took place. The proof that they happened and that they were perpetrated by the Presbytery is shown by a passage in the Kirk Session Records of Auchterhouse:

> *April 27th, 1669.* By the orders of the Presbytery of Dundee, action was ordered to be taken against all guilty of witchcraft. The Magistrates of Dundee were particularly desired to use all dilligence for trying them further. They complied with the Presbytery's instruc-tions, and appointed those suspected of witchcraft to be banished, which was done and the act put in execu-tion.

The Presbytery tried to conceal the matter, especially when it pertained to the execution of Grissel Jaffrey. They kept no records and asserted that the burning of Grissel Jaffrey was a myth – 'a popular delusion which had no basis in fact'. However, in the first decade of this century the Chief Librarian of Dundee wrote that he had discovered 'authentic documents now preserved in the Charter Room of Dundee' which threw some light on the old woman and her judges.

> . . . She was more acute than her neighbours in 'discerning the signs of the times', and could foretell disaster or good-luck by the exercise of her judge-ment . . . But the rage for witch-finding which infected the whole country took possession of three ministers of Dundee – Henry Scrymsour of St Mary's; John Guthrie, of the South Church; and William Rait, of the Third Charge, now St Paul's. Those were the leading ministers in the Presbytery of Dundee, and the reputa-tion of Grissel Jaffrey as a 'wise woman' came before them at an unfortunate time . . . The destruction of the

Presbytery Records, or at least, their silence, prevents us from knowing what actions were brought against this grey-haired old woman. We cannot tell what protracted examinations were made, what means were adopted to extort confessions of witchcraft from her, or what mental and physical torture she had to undergo to force her to accuse her comrades and neighbours. One thing is certain beyond dispute. The ministers declared her to be guilty of witchcraft.

If she did confess she undoubtedly underwent torture – why confess otherwise when, in those days, confession inevitably led to the stake? It would certainly have taken torture to extract the names of her 'accomplices'.

The Charter Room records state that she was kept prisoner in Dundee's tolbooth while awaiting trial. On 11 November 1669, the Privy Council, hearing the allegations, issued an order for her trial. 'Their remit to the Town Council and Presbytery was quite humane':

> . . . if by her own confession, without any sort of torture or other indirect means used, it shall be found she hath renounced her baptism, entered into paction with the Devil, or otherwise that malefices be legally proven

against her, that then and no otherwise the cause the sentence of death be executed upon her.

Apparently neither heeded it. No record of Grissel's trial exists in the Town Council minutes for 1669; they did as good a cover-up job as the clergy. But there is no doubt that it was originally recorded in the Town Council minutes because Thomson's *History of Dundee* (1874 edition) quotes from it:

> Dundie, the twenty-third day of November, 1669.
> Anent such as are delated for witchcraft: – The Ministers having also reported to the Counsell that Gryssel Jaffrey, witch, at her execution, did delate severall persons as being guiltie of witchcraft to them, and therefore desyred that for their exoneration some course might be taken against those delated. The Counsell in order thereunto nominates the Provost the present Baillies, the old Baillies, the Deane of Gild, and others to meet with the ministers, and to commune with them on the said matter, and to consider of the best wayes may be taken with the delated.

As the aforementioned Chief Librarian of Dundee wrote, 'Here it is shown that Grissel Jaffrey was actually tried and executed and that the ministers were still thirsting for the blood of other witch-martyrs.' Furthermore, Town Council records of 30 November 1669 show that Grissel's husband was admitted into the 'hospital' (the poorhouse) soon after her execution. This information, together with the fact that her story persists to this day in Dundee, shows Grissel's execution to be more than a 'popular delusion'.

In 1850 when a building was excavated in the Seagate – more approximately where the first Mercat Cross stood in Grissel's day and where felons were executed – a local rumour arose that a mound of ashes was found there. Dundonians, naturally, claimed they were Grissel's remains.

Grissel Jaffrey's execution remains a mystery. As there was so much of a cover-up most of what we know of it is hearsay. The most common story regarding the actual execution, handed down through generations of Dundonians, smacks of fiction. However, judge for yourself what truth there is in it. The story goes, that while the first faggots on the pyre were being lit and as Grissel screamed her innocence, a young sailor left his ship to visit the town. The sailor was a Dundonian who had left home to make his fortune at sea some years previously. Now that he had returned he wished to help his poor parents with whom he had had no contact since his departure. On seeing the townsfolk hurrying in droves towards the Seagate, he asked someone the reason for their haste. When he heard that the burning of a witch was starting he ran along with the throng. He reached the pyre to discover to his horror that it was his own mother at the stake.

The young man witnessed the execution – and, presumably, made it known to those about him who he was – then returned to his ship. As it sailed out of the River Tay, so the story goes, he cursed Dundee and all its citizens, vowing never to return.

MacPherson's Farewell
James MacPherson

> Farewell, ye dungeons dark and strong,
> The wretch's destinie!
> MacPherson's time will no' be long
> On yonder gallows-tree.

James MacPherson, the notorious freebooter immortalised in the famous song by Robert Burns, was hanged on the morning of 16 November 1700, eight days after his trial. The execution took place in Banff, and not in Inverness as Burns and Sir Walter Scott averred.

Burns' song is based on earlier versions, one of which is supposed to have been written by MacPherson himself. There is a tradition that a young woman from a respectable family developed an inseparable attachment to him. After witnessing his hanging she returned to the gypsy life to which MacPherson had brought her, singing the song he is supposed to have composed wherever she wandered.

However, this story is at variance with another, which claims he had 'a wife an' bairns', and there appears to be as many theories about his end as there are versions of the song. One story claims he was betrayed to the authorities by a lover:

> I've lived a life of sturt and strife;
> I die by trecherie;
> It burns my heart I must depart
> And not avenged be.

This story confuses MacPherson's final capture with the time when a gypsy girl unintentionally betrayed him to the authorities in Aberdeen. The girl was bribed to lure him into the city, but as soon as he was captured she alerted his comrades, claiming that the magistrates told her they only wanted to hear him play the violin, for he was a skilled performer. With the help of his friends, MacPherson escaped his gaolers.

Burns' editor, William Motherwell, attributes these conflicting stories to 'the unsettled way of the gypsy tribe to which MacPherson belonged' because 'they were allowed the same indulgences as the patriarchs of old – polygamy, or a plurality of wives and concubines . . .'

Other equally fictitious tales have grown around the last morning of MacPherson's life. The most common one maintains that the execution was hurried on by the magistrates when they received intelligence that the notorious freebooter was to be pardoned. They took many precautions to delay the messenger with the reprieve on his journey and put the town's main clock forward so that MacPherson would be hanged an hour before the appointed time. According to this story, the town of Banff was subsequently deprived of the power of trying and executing criminals because of this injustice.

The true story is dramatic enough as it stands. The magistrates *did* behave unjustly. On 8 November 1700, the Banff Magistrate Nicolas Dunbar passed sentence:

> Forasmeikle as you James MacPherson and James Gordon, pannels, are found guilty, by an verdict of as assyze, to be known, holden, and repute to be Egyptians and vagabonds, and oppressors of his majesty's free lieges, in a bangstree manner, and going up and down the country armed, and keeping markets in an hostile manner; and that you are theives, and that you are of *pessima fama*: Therefore the sheriff-depute of Banff, and I in his name, adjudges and decerns you, the saids James MacPherson and James Gordon, to be taken to the Cross of Banff, from the tolbooth thereof, where you now ly, and there, upon ane gibbet to be erected, to be hanged by the neck to the death, by the hand of the common executioner, upon Friday next, being the 16th November instant, being a public weekly market-day, betwixt the hours of two and three in the afternoon; and in the meantime, declares their haill moveable goods and gear to be escheat and inbrought to the fiscal, for his majesty's interest; and recommends this sentence to be seen put in execution by the magistrates of Bannf.

The magistrates ordered the execution for eight days after the trial, yet the Brown brothers, with whom he was arrested, were allowed to remain in gaol for over a year before escaping. MacPherson did not even belong to their gang. 'He was merely found in their company in pursuit of a gypsy wench of whom he was very fond.'

Indeed, another version of the story, which may be true, claims that MacPherson was betrayed to the authorities by his companions in revenge for stopping them from robbing the house of a wealthy gentleman. MacPherson, it is claimed, was incensed at their callousness because the gentleman's wife and two children were dead and still in the house waiting to be buried.

On the day of the execution the magistrates may have heard some rumour that MacPherson was to be reprieved because, although his death sentence was set for 'betwixt the hours of two and three in the afternoon', he was hanged in the morning. Their haste in executing him may have been due in part to the fact that he had been sprung out of gaol by fellow bandits once before and they were worried that an attempt might be made to free him again.

As he was led out to the gallows by the Banff Cross he was permitted to take his violin and play it. After playing *MacPherson's Rant* and *MacPherson's Pibroch* he asked if there was a friend in the crowd who would accept his trusty fiddle, 'his solace in many a gloomy hour', as a parting gift.

It would have been foolhardy for anyone to take up the offer. The magistrates at hand would have regarded such an act as 'acquaintance with a felon'. As MacPherson was a notorious criminal this would have had serious consequences. When he received no reply, MacPherson asserted that his companion would perish with him, broke the violin over his knee and threw away the fragments. With (as one version of the ballad called it) 'undaunted courage' he put his head through the noose. He was buried under the spot where the gallows stood.

After the crowd had dispersed Donald MacPherson, a close relation, picked up the neck of the violin. It is to this day preserved as a valuable memento of the family of Cluny, chieftain of the MacPhersons.

This was the last hanging in Scotland under the Heritable Jurisdiction System.

The Diabolical Doctor:
Glasgow's Last Public Execution
Dr Pritchard

There is no murderer, as one of the biographers put it, 'quite so loathsome' as Dr Edward William Pritchard, the last man to be publicly executed in Glasgow on 28 July 1865. It has been said that the only motive for his murders was fun, that he got pleasure out of killing his victims – of whom there were at least three.

When a fire broke out in his house in Glasgow's Berkeley Street, burning his servant girl to a 'charred mess', Dr Pritchard answered the door to a policeman who had spotted the flames. He told him that his son's cries of a fire had just woken him. This must have surprised the officer because the doctor was fully dressed. Soon after, the doctor, who had the house insured, claimed for articles of jewellery that could not be found in the debris. He eventually accepted an amount far below his original claim.

Further suspicion was aroused by the fact that Mrs Pritchard and the other servants were not in the house that night *and* it was the one night when the doctor had not checked with the girl whether he had been required for surgery. However, it was not until after Dr Pritchard had been charged with two other murders that journalists questioned why the girl had not escaped through the door quite close to her bed. If she had been asphyxiated by fumes there would have been some 'contraction or contortion' in the charred corpse. There was not. The conclusion at which the press belatedly arrived was that the girl either died before the fire started or was heavily drugged.

At the time of the fire rumours circulated that the girl was pregnant by Pritchard. These probably originated in other stories that reached Glasgow regarding his amorous adventures in England. (A scion of a distinguished naval and medical family, he was originally from Hampshire. He and his Scots wife left his Yorkshire practice to move to Glasgow in 1860.)

Soon after the fire incident the family moved and took on a new servant, an attractive 15-year-old girl called Mary McLeod. She not only replaced Elizabeth McGirn, the incinerated girl, as a servant, she also became the object of Pritchard's sexual advances.

She was more fortunate. He did not try to get rid of her by murder, but by accusing her of the murder of the two women he poisoned.

He was once charged with making sexual advances towards a woman but this was dropped because of 'adverse circumstances overtaking the gentleman whose wife had been insulted'. To make matters worse, Mary McLeod became pregnant. He kept her quiet by promising to marry her if his wife died before he did.

His wife knew of his affairs. She caught him kissing the girl often enough and had long arguments and rows over it. Although she idolised and kept him, she knew full well that she could not trust this tall, balding but handsome man. (He also wore a long beard but no moustache.) He was detested by every single member of the medical profession in Glasgow and was such a notorious liar that the letters of recommendation he had received from eminent men in his profession were rejected outright as forgeries. His wife, blinded by infatuation, ignored these things. She continually supplied him with money and in gratitude he poisoned her.

He began poisoning her in October 1864 with large amounts of deadly toxin. She suffered excruciating pain and delirium for five months before she died. When her worried mother – who idolised Pritchard – visited her, she too was poisoned. After staying in Berkeley Square for eleven days, she died in terrible agony.

At 1 a.m. on the morning of 18 March 1865, after he had refused her medicine prescribed by another doctor, his wife passed away. The medicine could hardly have acted as an antidote against all the poisons he had pumped into his wife over five months – Pritchard had more poisons in his home than had all the other doctors on Glasgow put together.

When his wife lay dead before him he burst into tears, crying, 'Come back, come back, my darling, Mary Jane. Do not leave your dear Edward.' The show was put on for the cook who was standing at the deathbed with Mary McLeod. He later wrote the death certificate, saying his wife died from gastric fever.

That same morning the procurator fiscal in Glasgow received a letter signed *Amor Justice*. It may well have

been written by the doctor who prescribed the drugs for Pritchard's wife on the night of her death. He had been called to the house by Mrs Pritchard a couple of times, but whenever he arrived either she would be too weak to tell him something she evidently wished to convey to him or she would remain silent because her husband was there. Perhaps she knew she was being poisoned. Certainly, the doctor must have had suspicions as he had attended Mrs Pritchard's dying mother. He would also have known of the unanimous contempt in which Pritchard was held by the members of Glasgow's medical profession. So it seems likely that he did write the letter – though he later denied it.

Sir,
    Dr Pritchard's Mother-in-law died suddenly and unexpectedly about 3 weeks ago in his house in Sauchiehall Street Glasgow under circumstances at least very suspicious.

His wife died today also suddenly and unexpectedly and under circumstances equally suspicious. We think it right to draw your attention to the above as the proper [unclear] to take action in the [unclear] and see justice done.

Unaware of what had passed, Pritchard met a lady friend in Sauchiehall Street and, in a chirpy manner, told her of his wife's death. Then he went to Edinburgh to arrange the funeral, at which he put on a show for his wife's family, kissing the lips of the corpse as it lay in the coffin. On his return journey, he astonished another passenger on the train by insisting he accept a photograph of him. He stepped on to the platform of Queen Street in a happy frame of mind. His mood changed instantly when Superintendent McCall stopped him, cautioned him and then arrested him on the grounds of murdering his wife. Eight days later, after examination, Mrs Pritchard's body was shown to be full of antimony, a dangerous poison. The authorities then decided to exhume her mother's body and similar poisons were found there.

The doctor remained quite calm and maintained his innocence when he was presented with these facts. He kept up the same calm demeanour and the protestations of innocence right to the gallows. Only twice did he show any signs of losing his nerve. The first time was when he had to put on a prison uniform; the second, when he was refused permission to trim his beard and hair.

The last person to be publicly hanged in Glasgow walked to the executioner holding a photograph of a family group including his wife, mother-in-law, two sons and three daughters. He often showed it to the warders or any of the other prisoners who cared to look at it.

ASSASSINATIONS . . .

Murder on the Altar Steps
John Comyn, Lord of Badenoch

When John Comyn, Lord of Badenoch, was murdered by Bruce in the Church of the Minorite Friars
at Dumfries, all Europe heard the cry of 'abomination'. 'The heinousness of the affair was its sacrilege;
twenty murders elsewhere were then held as nothing
to one death in the church, or one blow at the altar.'
Indeed, so strong was the taboo against committing an
act of violence in the house of God, that churches were
regarded as places of sanctuary.

Bruce was to pay dearly for his detestable crime. The
tyrannical Edward I swore on two swans clothed in gold
that 'dead or alive' he would enter Scotland and avenge
Comyn's murder; that he would take no rest 'until the
Lord has given me victory over the crowned traitor and
perjured nation'.

In Edward's plan Bruce and his accomplices were to
die as Wallace had; their estates were to be forfeited;
and Bruce's lands were to be divided amongst English
border lords. Many of Bruce's own lords deserted him
out of fear of Edward's wrath. Some even joined the
Comyn revolts led by the Lord of Badenoch's relatives.
MacDougal of Lorn gathered an army of Gaels against
him. Bruce lost battles at Perth and Methven, once flee-
ing in nothing but his shirt. His rash act had thrown the
nation into turmoil and turned him into a fugitive. However, if we are to understand why it happened, we must
look to what led to the murder.

John Comyn, known as the Red Comyn, held a
claim to the Scottish throne. So did Bruce. As Balliol's
nephew, and as one who up till then had done more to
the nation's cause than Bruce, Comyn had the greater
claim. However, this is not why Bruce slew him.

The Scots had been humiliated by Balliol. A pathetic
apology for a King, he was nicknamed Toom Tabard
('empty jacket') by his disgusted subjects. He bruised
Scotland's pride again and again by his weak-kneed
submission to Edward. Balliol had only accepted the
crown in the first place as Edward's vassal. In the four
years of Toom Tabard's rule, Edward relieved Scotland

of the Black Rod from Holyrood as well as whatever he wanted from Edinburgh Castle. He also took the country's prize possession, the coronation stone from Scone (believed to have been the very stone on which the Patriarch Jacob rested his head at Bethel in the Book of Genesis), and carried off the Annals of the Kingdom. In 1296 Balliol surrendered Scotland's throne to Edward and retired to his French estates.

From 1297 to 1305 Scotland had a great leader in Wallace. He restored the nation's badly wounded pride by his armed resistance to English rule. But after Edward had witnessed – and enjoyed – his final defeat, Scotland sank into a condition 'such as might even turn a coward's blood to flame'. English soldiers garrisoned every castle and town; English sheriffs and officers held power and legislated in every district. Their arrogance was such that 'men's lives were a misery to bear'. If an Englishman wanted a Scot's horse or hound, he simply took it. Women, young and old alike, were insulted in the streets by the invaders and any man who showed resentment of this treatment paid with his life. 'Many good knights were hanged like felons on the shallowest pretext, or none. The land was full of bitter wrong and shameful scorn.'

In great secrecy Bruce arranged a conspiracy for the overthrow of the English. He met Comyn and, while they were riding from Stirling, proffered the idea: 'Give me your land and I will assist you to expel the enemies, and place the crown on your head. Or else I will give you my lands on the condition that you support me in my efforts to regain the throne of my fathers.' Comyn agreed to the latter suggestion. A formal agreement was written out and each kept a copy.

Bruce then returned to England. He could never remain long from Edward's court because the English King mistrusted him and would not allow him long periods of leave – especially in Scotland. Meanwhile, Comyn had sent his copy of the deal to Edward, hoping to win favour through the betrayal. Edward affected to know nothing of Bruce's intentions when he appeared at court. But Bruce was sent a purse and a pair of spurs as a warning from his friend Gloucester. Taking the hint, he fled north the following morning. Two of his followers reversed his horse's shoes so it would look like they were leading to, rather than from, London.

The fugitive finally stopped at Lochmaben, his brother

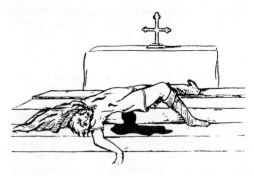

Edward's castle. He discovered there that the English were holding an assize court at Dumfries the following day. Comyn was to be there. Bruce, accompanied by friends, rode over to meet him.

The exchange in the Greyfriars' church started off cordially enough. They embraced and kissed each other as was the custom. But, as they walked down the aisle in serious discourse, their words became heated. By the time they reached the altar they were shouting at each other, Bruce accusing Comyn of betraying him to Edward. 'You lie,' Comyn yelled impudently. They were to be his last words. Bruce, in a fit of rage and almost without thinking, drew his dagger and struck him.

Instantly realising the rashness of his deed, he rushed outside to his waiting friends and confessed, 'I doubt that I have slain the Red Comyn.' Sir Roger Kirkpatrick, a staunch supporter of Bruce who was outraged by Comyn's treachery, said 'You doubt? I'll mak' siccar.' He ran into the church to make sure: if Comyn was not killed by Bruce's dagger, he was certainly killed by Sir Roger's sword.

Comyn himself must bear some of the responsibility for this outrageous crime. No man deserves to be murdered, but if anyone did it would have been Comyn. He betrayed his friend and his nation for his own selfish ends. The man he betrayed, it seems, had more altruistic reasons for pursuing Scotland's crown.

The First Regicide
James I

During the reign of James I (1394-1437) the Highlands 'had fallen into a state of lawlessness and disorder almost passing belief'. Clan battles were bloody in the extreme; after one battle at Strathnaver in Caithness only nine out of the 1200 men who went into battle survived. James himself twice led an army to put down violence and chaos. He reacted to the anarchy with enthusiasm. During his second Highland expedition he arrested 300 of the most notorious robbers. The spectacle of these fettered desperadoes marching through the streets achieved its aim: a deepening respect for the law. They were hanged to the last man.

A *ketheran*, or robber chief, was another recipient of James' speedy and stringent justice. He had plundered the home of a Highland widow, leaving her utterly destitute. When she swore to him that she would never again wear shoes till she had personally reported this violation to the King, he told her, 'It shall be a broken vow. You *shall* have shoes on your feet before you leave this spot.' Then he ordered his men to nail horseshoes to her bare soles.

The brutal act only made the woman more resolved. She made her way to the court and the King gave her an audience. After hearing her complaint and seeing the scars on her feet, James reacted instantly. He commanded the sheriff of the county where the outrage happened to seize the chief and deliver him to the King. The sheriff was given a particularly compelling reason not to allow the criminal to escape: he would be executed in the *ketheran*'s place if he did.

The felon was soon caught and sent to the King in Perth. He ordered an immediate execution. The chief was hanged in a shirt made especially for the occasion. On it was painted a picture of a Highlander nailing horseshoes on a woman's bare feet.

James 'the poet King' could be very tough when required. It was during his reign, in 1432, that Paul Crawar was burned at the stake in St Andrews for preaching the reformed doctrines. Crawar, a physi-

cian from Bohemia, had a brass ball bound into his
mouth to prevent him from preaching while he burned.
Nevertheless, James' toughness was generally tempered
with fairness. He brought peace and stability to a nation
that could recollect little or nothing of either. But his
severity brought about his own undoing.

As a result of his swift justice the country enjoyed 17
years of prosperity and the common people enjoyed a
happy period of comfort and security. Unfortunately for
the King this was achieved at the nobility's expense. He
reduced their power and bridled their lawlessness; he
forced some of the most powerful of them to surrender estates they had held without sufficient title. They
resented him bitterly. Violence and rapine had been
their trade and delight. That James' rule of law brought
prosperity to the nation at large did not placate them;
rather, it incensed them for they despised the common people. So they cherished revenge. James was a
marked man.

A conspiracy was hatched. The chief actor in it was
Sir Robert Graham, 'a dark, crafty, determined man'.
He was so determined that he once dared to propose
in open parliament that the King be arrested and imprisoned. Not surprisingly, the King reacted by confiscating
all his lands. But this only increased Graham's desire
for revenge. The Earl of Athole and Robert Stewart, the
King's Chamberlain, were his partners in treason.

In 1436, when James went to keep Christmas at the
Dominican friary in Perth, he encountered a Highland
woman at the Forth. She warned him that he would
never return. This was a frequently repeated warning
in Scots history; unfortunately, it was just as frequently
ignored. So with James. He rode on to Perth. The
woman followed regardless, repeating her warnings
along the way.

The night of 20 February 1497 had been a particularly
happy one for the residents of Perth friary. The King,
Queen and the ladies-in-waiting had enjoyed themselves playing chess and other evening games. They
had been entertained by reciters of literary romances, by
singers and a harpist. Even the Highland woman turned
up. She remained in the chamber after the entertainers
had left: the King was amused by her latest warnings and
stories of omens and premonitions. Suddenly, a great
clanking of armour was heard and James ceased to be
amused. From the windows they could see the glare of

torches lighting up the garden below. Stewart had lain planks over the moat for the conspirators to cross.

The Queen and her ladies tried to secure the doors, but there were no bolts – Stewart had removed them earlier. The King attempted to remove the bars from the window but they were stuck fast. At this the King, as one chronicle says, 'was ugly astonished, and in his mind could think of no other succour, but started to the chimney, and took the tongs, and under his feet he mightily burst up a plank of the chamber floor, and therewith covered him again, and entered adown low beneath.' This way led into a vault on the ground level. It had an opening into the garden through which he might have escaped had he not, only three days before, ordered the opening to be sealed – to stop tennis balls running through it when he played.

However, he got the women to lay the planks back across the vault entrance as best they could. Just as the conspirators drew near, one of the ladies, Catherine Douglas, thrust her arms through the iron staples of the door where the bolts had been. Her arm was soon smashed to bits as they forced their way through.

At first the King's pursuers thought he had escaped, but Catherine Douglas' brave but foolhardy act must have made them realise he could not be far away. Then one who was familiar with the place remembered the vault. He noticed the planks had been disturbed. He lifted them and thrust his torch into the vault. There he saw the King. He called out in delight, 'Sirs, the bridegroom is found for whom we have sought all the night.'

Sir John Hall leapt into the vault armed with a large knife. The defenceless King managed to throw him to the ground, but Hall's brother attacked him next. James' hands were badly slashed and mangled with attempting to grab the knives. Even then, the brave King managed to throw the second Hall to the ground. Graham was next to attack the King who was by now weary and faint. As he sprang at him, sword in hand, James cried for mercy. When Graham said he would receive none, the King said, 'I beseech thee then that for the salvation of my soul ye will let me hae a confessor.' 'Nae confessor shalt thou hae but this sword,' was Graham's retort as he ran it through the monarch's chest.

The Halls then began stabbing the King. Afterwards 16 deadly gashes were counted on the corpse's chest. Another 12 deep wounds were found on other parts. This despicable, cowardly murder was the first assassination of a Stewart monarch. It was a blunder besides. Whatever the nobles thought of the King, he was the idol of the common people. The Queen's vengeance had the sanction of the people and nothing is so relentless as popular fury. The burghers of Perth speedily rallied to the cause, 'St Johnstoun's hunt is up', and the pursuit was too hot for escape. Within a month the assassins were all caught and executed. Their ends were more gory and barbaric than the King's by far.

Slain by a Priest
James III

James was an unlucky name for Scots kings: James I was brutally assassinated; James II suffered a violent death at the siege of Roxburgh when a Scots cannon exploded and a fragment struck his groin, killing him instantly; James IV fell on Flodden Field with the flower of his nation – 25 lords, two prelates and 10000 men; and James V died in grief after the debacle at Solway Moss where his army was broken and scattered, many perished and over 1000 were taken prisoner.

James III (1451-88) was no less a tragic King than his namesakes. He was only seven years old when he succeeded to the throne. Bishop Kennedy ruled in the King's stead until he died in 1465 when James was only about 13. Power then passed to Robert, Lord Boyd, and his brother Alexander who, after coaxing the King from his palace in Linlithgow to Edinburgh, kept him a virtual prisoner.

But their decline was as rapid as their rise. The King had supporters and Lord Boyd fled; his brother Alexander was executed. When Lord Boyd's son, the Earl of Arran, returned to Scotland after his marriage to Princess Margaret of Denmark, he was informed of the situation. Refusing to disembark, he and his wife at once set sail for Denmark.

Though not a particularly bad King, James III ruled unwisely. He earned the emnity of his rude and unlettered nobles by preferring the company of men of refinement, taste and dexterity – artists, craftsmen and men of mechanical skill. Ironically, his illiterate, uncouth nobles were extremely snobbish and regarded those erudite men who enjoyed the King's patronage as their social inferiors. They complained that the King's favourites were 'masons and fiddlers'. Considering the hostility of his nobles, it was unwise of James to make these favourites his leisure companions, but it was the utmost folly to make them his advisers. And that he did.

His prime favourite was Cochrane, a mason and a gifted architect who designed the great hall of Stirling Castle. The other favourites were Rogers, a musician;

Torpichen, a dancing master; Andrews, a tailor; and Leonard who was a smith or a shoemaker.

James conferred his dead brother's earldom on Cochrane. His nobles were galled; they detested Cochrane because he lived in splendour and pomp that eclipsed the proudest amongst them. It's said that all places of honour were given through his favour. Whoever wanted court influence or protection had to buy it from him. '. . . no man got audience of the King but by this means, or by giving him gear, which, if they did, their matters went right, were they just or unjust . . . So the wise lords' counsels were refused, and their sons absent from the King's service.'

Cochrane is supposed to have caused division between James and his brothers who were popular men. When one of them − John, Earl of Mar − died, the other, Albany, was accused of witchcraft and imprisoned in Edinburgh Castle. However, he escaped to his own castle at Dunbar. From there Albany fled to France and then to England where he swore fealty to Edward on the condition that he would undertake to make Albany the King of Scotland.

About this time the English had marched an army to the border and the Scots mobilised in reply for 'resisting the reiver Edward calling himself the King of England'. One of the largest armies ever raised in Scotland mustered on the Boroughmuir at Morningside, Edinburgh. James, as if to infuriate his nobles further, made Cochrane manager of the guns.

This was a turning-point for the nobles. They resolved to overthrow the favourites and bring the King under their own guidance. Camped at Lauder Bridge they discussed their plot in a nearby church. There Lord Gray related the fable of the cat and the mice. The mice thought that a bell tied to the cat's neck, giving warning of its approach, would greatly enhance their own safety. But the scheme failed due to the lack of a mouse bold enough to bell the cat.

'I understand the moral,' said the Earl of Angus, 'and what ye propose micht nae lack execution. I will bell the cat.' From then on he was known as Bell-the-Cat.

Just as this was said there was a knock at the door. They demanded who it was.

'It is I, the Earl of Mar,' said Cochrane, strutting in haughtily.

He was dressed in a doublet of black velvet 'with ane

great chain of gold about his neck, to the value of 500 crowns; and ane ane fair blowing horn, in ane chain of gold, borne and tipped with fine gold at both ends, and ane precious stone called ane beryl hanging at the ends thereof'.

Angus pulled the chain from him saying, 'A rope wad serve ye better.'

Then Douglas of Lochleven snatched the horn, telling him that he had been 'the hunter of mischief for too lang'.

'My lords,' he asked, 'is this jest in earnest?'

'It is guid earnest and so shalt thou find.'

At once the conspirators despatched a group of armed men to secure the King and seize the rest of his favourites. Then they bound Cochrane's hands with rope. Vain to the last, he begged them to take a silken cord from his tent and save him the disgrace of being bound with a hempen rope like a common thief. The contemptuous lords retorted that as a traitor he deserved no better. He was taken to the bridge and then hung in front of the King's eyes. The rest of the King's favourites, except for one, were hanged beside him. The King's entreaties managed to save the life of Ramsay, a youth of 17.

The lords expected to pay for this. Certain the King was waiting for his hour of vengeance, they were too fierce to sit by idly and wait for James to act first. They saw their choice: either wait for destruction or once more bell the cat. They chose the latter. They mustered their forces and rose in armed rebellion.

The prince, a 17-year-old boy, was told by the rebels that his father had forfeited the crown. They then proclaimed him King, under the title of James IV.

The armies met not far from Bannockburn. The cruellest blow for James was the intelligence he had received that his son was among the mortal enemies. What would become of his son if his side were losing? Would the nobles slay him in their anger? It was a bitter day for the King.

The battle was not long begun when what little courage James had deserted him. He copied his courage and deserted from the field, spurring his steed through the village of Bannockburn. Seeing an armed horseman at full gallop, a woman drawing water from the burn threw down her pitcher and ran off. The horse was startled and bound across the stream, throwing the King off at the mill door. Bruised badly both by the fall and the weight of the armour, he passed out.

The miller and his wife took him into the mill and laid him in a corner under a blanket. When he eventually came to, he asked the miller if there was a priest nearby to whom he could confess. The miller asked who he was. 'I was your King this morning,' he replied. At that the wife ran outside, clapping her hands and shouting, 'A priest for the King!'

Before long a man ran in claiming to be a priest and asking for the King. (According to some sources the man was dressed as a priest and some have believed he was indeed a priest – for what other reason would he have been dressed as one?) He knelt, asking how the King fared and if he thought he would recover. The King said he believed he should but in the meantime desired to make a confession.

The man leaned over the King as if to help keep his confession from the ears of the miller and his wife. As James quietly began confessing the stranger pulled out a dagger and stabbed the 35-year-old King five times about the heart.

He departed as quickly as he came and was never caught. Whence he came, or where he went, history has no record.

The Bludy Serk
Cardinal Beaton

Cardinal Beaton's cruelty was notorious. That and his
wanton pomp did more for the Protestant cause in Scotland than the preaching of martyrs such as Hamilton
and George Wishart.

The unjust and cruel death of Wishart – burned at
the stake as Cardinal Beaton looked on, reclining on
luxurious cushions, from the keep of his castle – was
the last straw for some Reformers. Wishart had been
burnt at Beaton's instigation after an irregular trial and
without even the sanction of the civil power. Now the
Reformers decided to react in kind.

Some building had been going on in the Cardinal's
castle at St Andrews and on the morning of 29 May
1546 Norman Leslie, son of Lord Rothes, and another
two men entered the grounds with the masons and
other workmen. Then James Melville, followed by three
others, approached the gate and asked for an interview
with the Cardinal. The porter became alarmed when
Kirkcaldy of Grange arrived with eight armed men to
give Melville backing. He must have either tried to flee
and warn Beaton, or refused to admit them, for he was
stabbed and thrown into the moat.

Beaton, resting after having spent a night with his
concubine Marion Ogilvy, was roused by the commotion. His assassins burst in and held him at sword point,
demanding that he repent of the murder of George
Wishart. 'How dare you threaten to murder me,' he
screamed at them. 'I am a priest.' This was a red rag
to a bull. If they had thought of sparing him they were
reminded in their rage that here in front of them was a
priest of the Whore of Babylon, the church of antichrist,
an avowed opponent of the true gospel who had been
personally responsible for the death of Christ's martyrs.
To make matters worse he was quite unrepentant. Furious, they slew him on the spot.

Word of what happened reached townspeople.
Those who saw the Reformers, rather than the Cardi-
nal, as opponents of Christ's Gospel, marched with the
Provost to the castle walls. Led by the Provost, they

shouted for Cardinal Beaton. 'What hae ye done to my Lord Cardinal? Let me see my Lord Cardinal.'

Some of the conspirators appeared on the battlements and at the windows to tell the crowd that they were late in the day for the Cardinal 'would trouble the world no more'. This made the crowd more irritable and again they demanded to speak with the Cardinal. Norman Leslie shouted to them that they were unreasonable fools seeking to speak with a dead man. Still they demanded to see him. Leslie and his friends gave them their wish. They tied the bloody corpse by an arm and a leg with sheets and hung it over the battlements. The crowd recognised the gashed corpse in the blood-soaked garment as their Cardinal.

'Behold your God,' Leslie called to them. 'And now you are satisfied get ye hame to your houses.' This time the crowd obeyed – immediately.

Jealousy Cruel as the Grave
David Rizzio

David Rizzio, an Italian musician, entered the service of Mary Queen of Scots during a troubled time for the nation. Irish chiefs in rebellion against Elizabeth I, English Catholic nobles, and Philip of Spain all wanted Mary firmly established in Scotland, the Catholic Church restored and Elizabeth dethroned with Mary in her place. Philip made plans for such an event, hoping to root out Protestantism in Europe and form a 'Holy Roman Empire' under the Pope.

Being a devout Catholic, Mary was quite in sympathy with the idea. She herself signed the 'League' or 'Holy Union,' originally planned by her uncle the Cardinal of Lorraine. It was thought that she was pressured by Rizzio, an agent for the Pope, who had become her favourite and confidant. He was quickly promoted from musician to be employed in her private foreign correspondence. Proud of his position and influence he became vain and pompous.

Both because of the threat of Catholic domination of Europe, and of Rizzio's influence over the Queen, many of the Scottish Protestant lords feared for their lives. When they plotted Rizzio's death they found Mary's husband Darnley on their side – although he wanted Rizzio killed for more personal reasons. Mary's love for her husband had cooled within months of their marriage. Darnley, she discovered, was a libertine, a fop and a fool. She had every right to be bitter. Despite a host of gallant suitors she had announced her marriage to Darnley within three months of their first meeting. Now she made no attempt to hide her revulsion for Darnley, nor to hide her fondness for Rizzio. Understandably, Darnley was galled. 'He told of his grief and shame to his uncle, George Douglas, who told of it to another uncle, Lord Ruthven, and to his son.' These relatives wanted revenge.

Rizzio's death warrant was finally signed when Mary assembled a parliament to devise measures for the restoration of Catholicism in Scotland and for the punishment of lords in rebellion. Five days after that parliament, when darkness fell on the evening of Saturday 9 March 1566, the Earl of Morton and Lord Lindsay suddenly and quietly entered the courtyard of Holyrood Palace and closed the gates. They were armed and were attended by 150 men bearing torches.

Darnley led several men into his own room and took Ruthven by a secret stair into a small closet that was entered from the Queen's bedchamber. Ruthven and Darnley stormed into the Queen's chamber where she was dining with Lady Argyll, Rizzio and some attendants. They were all alarmed at Ruthven's appearance as he had risen from his sickbed and his eyes were blazing. It was common belief at the time that he dabbled in sorcery or black magic. Some of the Queen's company thought he was either delirious or possessed. To make matters worse, he was wearing a steel helmet and armour showed underneath his cloak.

The Queen stood up, demanded the meaning of the intrusion and, sensing the purpose of the visit, put herself between Ruthven and Rizzio – who clutched in terror at her dress. It was to be the last night he would sing for her.

Ruthven replied, 'Let yon man Davie cam forth frae your presence for he hath been ower lang there.' He then accused him of offending the Queen's honour – an understatement considering Rizzio's chambers were directly beneath hers and he was at liberty to come and go almost as he pleased. Mary then accused a somewhat embarrassed Darnley of his hand in the affair.

Rizzio shrank back and cowered in the window recess. When Ruthven lunged at him the Queen's attendants tried to intervene. At this point Ruthven cried out, 'Lay no' your hands on me for I will no' be handlit.' This was the signal for the accomplices, George Douglas, Andrew Ker of Fawdonside ('a tall, thin-made, resolute-looking man'), Patrick Bellenden, Thomas Scott and Henry Yair to rush in. Mary was again in front of Rizzio at the window recess trying to protect him. A table was knocked over in the mêlée and Lady Argyll caught the last candle, saving it from being extinguished. Had it gone out Rizzio might have made an escape.

Bellenden and Ker were wielding pistols, the others daggers, as they prised the Italian's hands from Mary's dress. Finally he was dragged from her, screaming and kicking violently.

Mary showed immense bravery for she expected to be murdered also. She believed Darnley had planned her murder and that of her unborn child – for she was six or seven months pregnant at the time. According to her own accusation after her son's birth, Fawdonside's pistol had been pointed at her belly. There must have been great vindictiveness in the minds of the assassins because they would have known that Rizzio's murder could have caused a miscarriage and few women survived them in those days.

However, as Rizzio was being dragged out, Ruthven, urging Darnley to take the Queen in his arms, told her not to be afraid as they would spend their heart's blood for her and were only doing her husband's bidding. Nevertheless, after the murder, Mary was left to spend the night alone without any kind of medical attention or even a midwife. Only Lady Huntly was allowed to remain with her. Thus it seems likely that the assassins hoped she would miscarry: her death would have secured their futures.

Mary could hear Rizzio's pathetic screams from the stairhead as the murderers thrust their daggers into his body: *'Justizia! Justizia! Sauvez ma vie, madame, sauvez ma vie!'* She was later convinced that the first blow was struck when he was behind her in the window recess, though it was denied by the assassins and their supporters. The first blow known to be struck was by George Douglas and with Darnley's dagger, perhaps to implicate him further.

Rizzio received between 50 and 60 deep wounds, a particularly frenzied butchery for a small body such as his. His torn and bleeding corpse was then thrown down the winding stairs – although the assassins' plan had originally been to take him to the Town Cross and hang him there.

A porter stripped the body of its belongings as it lay on a chest at the foot of the staircase. Like a Shakespearean actor, he moralised in soliloquy as he did so: 'This was his destiny for upon this chest was his first bed when he cam' to this place, and there he lieth, a very niggard and misknown knave.'

The cry ran throughout Edinburgh that a murder had been committed at the palace and the Queen kept prisoner inside. The Provost ordered the ringing of the common bell and, before long, about 500 armed burghers responded to its peal. When they reached the palace Darnley appeared at a window and ordered them to disperse and go home. He assured them that the Queen and he were both merry. (Mary tried to make her voice heard then, but Lindsay threatened to 'cut her in collops' if she took another step towards the window.) When the Provost asked to speak to the Queen, Darnley replied, 'Ken ye no' that I am King? I command ye to pass hame to your houses.' They did.

Later, when Ruthven and Darnley had departed, Mary sent one of her ladies-in-waiting to find out the news of Rizzio's fate. She returned to say that he was dead. Mary burst into tears but quickly restrained herself saying, 'No more tears now. I will think upon revenge.'

In the Dead of Night
Lord Darnley

Soon after the murder of Rizzio, Queen Mary was plotting the death of her husband. She was aided by her new favourite James Hepburn, the Earl of Bothwell, whom she raised to greater wealth and power than he already possessed. He was appointed High Admiral and received the rich abbey lands of Melrose and Haddington. He was also made Warden of the Marches although that office had previously been divided among three men, one for each of the three Marches.

As the Queen's lover, Bothwell wanted Darnley out of the way as much as she. He also wanted to be King. Darnley had become extremely unpopular due to his known involvement in Rizzio's murder and Mary and Bothwell no doubt began their plotting while public emnity was still prevalent.

On the night of Sunday 9 February 1567, the Queen went to visit her husband who was convalescing in his sickbed in Kirk o' the Field – the former Edinburgh residence of the Provost of the religious house of St Mary in the Fields which stood near to where the university now stands. Darnley had moved there on 31 January, after having been taken ill in Glasgow. At about 10 p.m. the Queen sat talking to him while the room directly beneath was being filled with bags of gunpowder by three of Bothwell's servants – his tailor, George Dalgliesh; his porter, William Powrie; and Patrick Wilson. As soon as the room was laid with all the explosives Bothwell's former servant, French Paris, went up to the King's room. It was a signal to Mary that all was ready. She recalled that she had to attend the revels at her favourite valet's wedding.

Darnley did not want her to go. He had been drinking wine and was in a sullen mood. According to Lennox, he even said to her, 'It was aboot this time of year that Rizzio died.' But Mary, determined to go, dealt with him as if he were a child. She promised to come back and gave him a ring as a pledge that she would. Reluctantly he accepted.

Mary did go to the ball. So did Bothwell. However, she did not stay long; a carriage took her back to Holyrood where she soon went to bed. Bothwell slipped out from the ball around midnight and changed his fancy clothes of velvet and satin for more common ones. He then joined his accomplices at Kirk o' the Field.

At 1 a.m. John Hepburn, a relation, lit the fuse and sneaked out of the house with fellow assassin John Hay of Talla. They met Bothwell in the garden and he asked them if they'd 'fixed the lunt?' When they told him 'It is done', they retired in the darkness with other accomplices and kinsmen to a safe distance. Some armed Douglases were also among them as there were among the accomplices at Rizzio's murder.

All was dark and still within the doomed house. Darnley slept as the last seconds of his life ticked away. The smouldering end of the fuse crept slowly towards the powder . . . The explosion seemed long in coming and they thought the fuse had gone out.

The impetuous Bothwell was all for going into the house and relighting the fuse. Hepburn, knowing the fuse was set properly, managed to get him to see sense. Just as well for Bothwell. Soon after, there was an explosion that blew the solid stone house to smithereens, from its roof to its foundations. The eruption lit the sky and its glow and noise could be seen and heard for miles. The conspirator Paris said that the air was rent by the 'crack' and that every hair on his head stood on end. Herries' *Memoirs* describe the blast as 'fearful to all about, and many rose from their beds at the noise'. The Queen in Holyrood was even awakened 'as if by the sound of thirty or forty cannon'. She sent messengers to find out what had happened (as if she did not already know) before going back to sleep.

The assassins fled the scene and Bothwell returned to his apartments in the palace, drank some wine and went to sleep. Meanwhile, terrified citizens roused themselves from their beds and ran to see what had happened. They found Nelson, one of Darnley's servants, on top of what was left of the town wall. He was still alive. They realised straight away that there had been an attempt on the King's life, but hoped to find Darnley also alive. Their hope was soon ended. In the orchard – where the force of the blast had flung them – lay the dead bodies of the King and his servant.

Strangely, there were no burn marks on the corpses. That gave birth to the idea that the explosion had not killed them and they had been strangled on the spot by their killers. This theory arose because a rope was found next to Darnley's body. But so were a chair, a dagger and a fur-lined cloak. It is not so surprising that the bodies were not scorched or blackened. The beds they had lain on would have protected them from the direct effect of the blast and it is more likely they were killed by the fall from the heights than by the explosion itself.

Morning came and the Queen ate a hale and hearty breakfast. When Darnley's corpse was brought to Holyrood chapel Mary 'beheld it without any outward sign of joy or sorrow'. The following Saturday she had the body interred secretly, and by night, in the chapel beside the remains of David Rizzio.

The outcry for Bothwell to be brought to justice grew too great for Mary to ignore. She gave orders for a public trial but it seemed as if she wished to make a mockery of the memory of her husband, for the jury consisted of Bothwell's partisans. Four thousand of his armed followers were in the city; no witnesses were summoned and the chief assassin rode to the trial on her murdered husband's favourite horse. As he passed the palace Mary stood at a window and waved to him. She publicly expressed her sympathy by sending him a token and a message when he was still before the judges.

They passed a unanimous verdict of acquittal. Mary had her revenge.

At Huntly's Heinous Hands
James Stewart, the second Earl of Moray

George Gordon, the sixth Earl of Huntly (1562-1636), was an unruly, troublesome Highland chief. His friends called him 'Cock o' the North', an appellation he thoroughly enjoyed, boasted of and certainly lived up to. He was king on his own estates. As far as he was concerned he had no king but Caesar and his Caesar was himself. He only showed acquiescence to the King – James VI – when it was to his own advantage.

Like many northern lords, he had Catholic sympathies. He was willing to admit the defeat of the Armada, and entered into a treasonable correspondence with Philip of Spain. When his letters were intercepted in England, the country he was plotting to invade, Elizabeth demanded immediate punishment.

King James was deeply worried to find that such a powerful lord as Huntly was the leader of this Catholic faction. It is likely that he did not want to believe in Huntly's treachery as it was his fancy that he had rescued him 'as a brand for the burning, from the clutches of Rome' and turned him into a good Protestant. However, because he did not have the power to defy Elizabeth, James had Huntly arrested and imprisoned in Edinburgh Castle. But it was not for long. Huntly was soon released and banished to his own lands in Strathbogie.

Huntly was soon in trouble again. He led a rebellion in the north that was backed in the south by the earls of Crawford, Errol and Bothwell. James, however, put down the rebellion and imprisoned Huntly. But it was again only for a short time. Huntly was soon free once more to carry on in his self-indulgent ways, crushing those imprudent enough to obstruct him. He was to be the main assassin involved in a bloody murder that is still remembered in one of our most melancholy ballads.

Ye Highlands and ye Lowlands
wherefore have ye been?
They hae slain the Earl o' Moray
An' hae lain him on the green!

James Stewart, the second Earl of Moray, had been Regent prior to James VI's accession to the throne. The son-in-law of the previous Regent, the first Earl (see page 11), he was gallant, young and handsome and known as 'the Bonnie Earl'. The King accused him of aiding and abetting Francis Hepburn, the fifth Earl of Bothwell, in a violent raid, and gave the commission for his arrest to Huntly who accepted it with relish. According to the ballad he *was* commanded to take Moray alive.

> Now wae be tae ye, Huntly,
> And wherefore did ye sae?
> I bade you bring him wi' you,
> But forbade you him to slay.

However it must have been obvious to James that Huntly had no intention of taking Moray alive. He was well aware of the feud between the Gordons and the Stewarts and knew that there was no love lost between Huntly and Moray themselves. So it seems likely that the King actually wanted Moray dead, perhaps because he thought there were some romantic inclinations between him and the Queen – the ballad calls him 'the queen's bonny lover'. Certainly it is strange that James should demand Moray's arrest while allowing Hepburn, the chief culprit, to go free – considering Hepburn was reckless, wicked, manic, perhaps mad, and believed to be a warlock ruling seven covens of witches.

Whatever the reason, the arrest offered Huntly an unexpected opportunity to humiliate a traditional enemy. He rode from Edinburgh with 400 Gordon horsemen, crossing at Queensferry to Donibristle (now Dunibirsell) Castle on the coast nearby. On arriving there late in the evening, he called up on the Earl to surrender. When the Earl refused, Huntly ordered his men to place nearby cornstacks against the massive door. These were then set alight.

The only people in the castle with Moray were his mother and sisters, Dunbar (the sheriff of Moray) and a few servants. Realising how desperate was their situation Dunbar hit on a plan: 'I will gae oot afore your lordship and I'm sure they will charge on me, thinking me your lordship. So, it being dark, you shall cam oot efter me, and look if ye can provide for yourself.'

The devoted man pushed open the burning door and sprang out, charging desperately among the Gordons.

They all turned on him, hacking and slashing till he was dead. While this savagery was taking place, Moray dashed out through the flames and smoke to hide in the rocks close by. He was unaware, though, that the tassel of his cap caught fire as he leapt through the flames. And, just as he thought he was safe, a faint glow from it betrayed him to some keen-eyed Gordons. They were on him in seconds.

Huntly struck the first blow, slashing at his face. Being a handsome and vain man it is possible that Huntly's vanity was stung through Moray being called 'the Bonnie Earl'. If so, the attack must have given him great delight. Moray himself must have seen this as a motive for, as the others were plunging their swords into him, he had a last taunt: 'Ye hae spoilt a better face than your ain, my lord!'

After the murder Moray's mother showed amazing magnanimity. The Gordons, stripping one of their own clansmen of his hat, sporran, weapons and stockings, left him for dead in front of her castle. Although he had helped to bereave the woman, she 'took him in and cherished him with every care that a wounded man requires'.

She had a gruesome painting made of her son's body, gashes and all, with a motto, 'God avenge my cause,' emitting from his mouth. (It presently hangs in Darnaway Castle, Morayshire.) She took it to the King and knelt before him, imploring justice. Fearing public opinion – which backed the clergy's demand that Huntly be pursued 'with fire and sword' – the King left Edinburgh for a while. The 'wae' he inflicted on Huntly was a week's imprisonment in Edinburgh Castle.

The King's Dastardly Deed
John, Earl of Gowrie, and
Alexander, Master of Ruthven

'The Gowrie Conspiracy' – as historians call the two assassinations that took place in Gowrie House, Perth, on 5 August 1600 – is one of Scotland's greatest murder mysteries. The protagonists included John Ruthven, Earl of Gowrie, his younger brother Alexander, Master of Ruthven, and James VI.

According to the King, Alexander Ruthven approached him at Falkland where he had been hunting and asked him back to Gowrie House to see a man who had been arrested in possession of a pot of gold. As soon as the King had dined at Gowrie House, Ruthven enticed him into an adjoining room in the tower in the house. There was no man with a pot of gold to be seen but an armed one who kept watch while Ruthven told the King he was to die and held a knife at his breast. The King, fighting him off, ran to the window and screamed 'Treason' whereupon James' servant, John Ramsay, ran into the room and slew Ruthven. The King then threw the body down the turnpike (the winding staircase in a turret). However, the tumult had alerted the Earl who, backed by some servants, ran into the room. He, too, was slain by the King's retainers.

Some historians have believed this version of the story; others have disputed it. It is highly unlikely that a timid man like James could struggle with a taller, stronger, and much younger man than himself. It is just as improbable that he, unarmed, could break away from the armed Ruthven, make for the window and cry treason, or that after Ruthven was slain, he would have the strength to throw the body down the stairs. James had 'a bodily weakness which almost amounted to infirmity'. Besides, what was Ruthven's armed man doing while all this was happening? If Ruthven wanted to kill the King he could have done it when the armed man was in the room. Moreover, if Ruthven and Gowrie had murder in mind, it is highly unlikely that they would have invited the King with 20 armed cavalrymen. The King later claimed that Ruthven had asked him to come alone, but it is still unlikely that the Ruthven brothers would attempt his life when they were so badly outnumbered. Furthermore, it took James about a month to publish this version of the story. It was not believed by the people of Perth, who nearly rioted when they heard that Gowrie had been slain. He was their Provost and they loved and respected him. They believed King James plotted his and his brother's murders. So did many of the clergy. They refused to preach the King's version of the story from their pulpits although it was a royal command to do so.

James had four of Gowrie's servants horribly tortured, and three of the four hanged, but none of them admitted to his version of what happened. One of Gowrie's household – Andrew Henderson – did, however, admit to being the armed man in the tower. The King had described the armed man as being 'tall dark and grim'. Interestingly, Henderson, who was neither tall nor dark but very ruddy, was pardoned and pensioned!

It is worth remembering that although he was timid and could not bear the sight of an unsheathed sword or dagger, James was notoriously cruel and callous in dispensing with those he wished to. He was unscrupulous in ambition and would go a great deal further than lying to secure it. Besides, despite their apparent loyalty, James had reason to fear the Ruthven brothers. They were grandsons of that grim murderer of David Rizzio and their father had been beheaded on James' orders 19 years earlier. Nineteen years could not erase from James' mind the virtual imprisonment he had experienced in their father's castle prior to executing him. The Ruthven brothers belonged to a family that had harried James before, and they had a motive for revenge.

Or perhaps jealousy was the inspiration behind the Gowrie House murders, as it may have been in the slaying of Moray? Reports of the time tell us that Gowrie was one of the Queen's favourites.

The fact that the King's version of the story conflicts with his accomplices' adds to its unacceptability. According to the King, Alexander Ruthven locked all the passage doors of Gowrie House behind him as he guided him through its halls. John Ramsay, who slew Ruthven, claimed, however, that he took the same route as the King and Ruthven soon after.

The theory current at the time is probably closest to

the truth, and it is likely that it was the King who asked Ruthven into the fateful room. Ruthven was said to have suspected he would be accused of attempting to murder the King and so, on entering the room, he immediately unsheathed his two swords and stuck them into the floorboards. Then Ramsay, who had entered the room by way of the turnpike, ran at him, stabbed him to death and threw his body down the stairs while James ran to the window and cried out, 'Treason, treason! Help, I am slain!'

Ramsay's claim was that on hearing 'a struggling and din of men's feet', he burst into the room. There he saw 'Master Alexander, being almost on his knees, had his hand upon his Majesty's face and mouth.' If this were true, why was Ruthven killed when he could have been arrested there and then and charged with treason? Clearly the King was bent on his death, because even if we accept that the struggle did take place, we have it on Ramsay's own testimony that the King's first words to him were, 'Fy! Strike him because he has a pyne dowlit [secret doublet] upon him.'

(Ramsay, younger brother to George, first Lord Ramsay of Dalhousie, had committed a murder a few months previously. He slew with his sword the Master Carver of Falkland. Though tried and found guilty of 'transgressing his Highnesses laws and acts of Parliament', he was only given a reprimand and kept his office as 'one of his Majesty's familiar servants'.)

As soon as he stabbed the Master of Ruthven, Ramsay ran to the window and shouted down to his accomplices, George Wilson and Dr Herries, who were standing in the courtyard, 'Cam up tae this turnpike even to the head.' When they ran up and arrived in the tower room he shouted, 'This is the traitor. Strike him!' In an instant their hunting knives had finished the work begun by Ramsay. As the master sank mortally wounded, he

cried with his last breath, 'Alace, I had nae wyte of it.'

Hearing a din coming from the tower room, the nobles Lennox, Mar and Gowrie ran towards it. Gowrie was obstructed by Sir Thomas Erskine and his brother James; the latter seized him by the throat crying, 'Traitor, is this thy wark?' 'What is the metter?' cried Gowrie. 'I ken naething.'

As he was thrown to the ground, his kinsman Ruthven of Forgan rushed towards Erskine and knocked him down. Thomas Cranston, a friend of Gowrie, ran to their aid.

The Earl's assailants ran to the tower turnpike — no doubt to report to the King that their assassination of Gowrie was foiled. Gowrie himself ran 'the space of half a pair of butt-lengths' and drew his two swords from their scabbards. Cranston, unsheathing his own sword and running with him, asked what the fight was about and what he should do. Gowrie replied, 'I will gang into my ain house or die by the way.' At that point a 'lacquey' appeared and tied a steel bonnet on his head.

Cranston, still following, asked, 'Pray, wha should I strike? I ken nae wha is pairtie.' But the Earl was himself unsure, although he must have had his suspicions.

They met several of his retainers who had been alerted by the tumult. Among them was Craigingelt who had seen the dead body of the Master of Ruthven and had armed himself with a large, two-handed sword. He ran with the other retainers to the back gate to halt the assassins' escape while Cranston and Gowrie ran up the turnpike stairs towards the tower room. James later claimed they had eight accomplices though other witnesses stated they were alone.

They ran past the dead body at the foot of the stairs though 'neither knew who it was nor whether he was hurt or dead:' On reaching the top they encountered Sir Thomas Erskine, Ramsay, Wilson and Herries. Herries lunged at Cranston with his sword. Cranston contented himself with parrying; he called to Herries, 'Theif, gif thou be innocent of yon slaughter, come forth and I will warrant ye.' Meanwhile, the Earl parried with Ramsay. Gowrie and Cranston were very skilled swordsmen and had they wished they could have easily slain their four opponents. Obviously they were intent on having these men arrested.

Although it is not mentioned in the official records, and none of the assassins ever admitted it, Captain Preston, the messenger sent to Queen Elizabeth with the report, tells us the logical ending to the fray. Unable to get the better of the two men, one of Gowrie's enemies cried out, 'The King is slain.' At this, 'the Earl shronke from the pursuit' and, seizing the opportunity, Ramsay 'rushed upon him suddenly and thrust him through that he fell and died'. Cranston was still putting up a brave fight despite his wounds, but on realising what had happened to his friend, he 'lap out at the dur and came forth of the place'. Wilson was the only one who escaped without a wound. Herries had two fingers hacked off by a blow from Cranston's sword.

After they had locked Gowrie's body in a closet the assassins went into the room where the King was at the top of the turnpike. Lennox, Mar and some others – all of whom were obviously in on the plot – were also admitted. When Ruthven of Forgan ascended the turnpike and realised Lennox was at the other side of the door, he pleaded, 'My lord, tell me how my Lord of Gowrie does.' Lennox replied that Gowrie was well and advised, 'Gang your way. Ye are a fool and will get little thanks for your labours.' Ruthven, apparently appeased by the news, departed.

> The Earl of Gowrie and the Master of Ruthven were both dead; their friends had retired; James was in the midst of his own servants, kneeling down on his knees, and they all kneeling round him, out of his own mouth he thanked God of that miraculous deliverance and victory, assuring himself that God had preserved him from so despaired a peril, for the perfiting of some greater work behind, to his glorie, and for procuring by him the weal of his people, that God had committed to his charge.

Only a King as cruel and callous as James could carry out such a dastardly deed and actually believe it had God's sanction.

... AND MURDERS

The Wolf of the North
Lord Badenoch

If Albany was bad enough Badenoch was as bad if not worse.

Alexander Stewart, a younger brother of Robert III and the Duke of Albany, could not be brought to heel by his powerful brothers. Powerful as Albany was, notorious for his rapacity and insolence, he could not control his younger brother. He may have ruled the rest of Scotland, including its King, but he did not rule Alexander Stewart, aptly nicknamed 'the Wolf' because he lived by the dictates of his unbridled passions. 'He was cruel and merciless as a wolf, sparing none; his fury fell upon all, Church, noble and burgher, but his epitaph reads, *"Bona Memoriae"*!' He was otherwise known by the Gaelic title of Alasdair Mór Mac an Rígh (Great Alexander, son of the king) for he was Robert II's bastard son; his mother, Elizabeth Muir, was the King's mistress whom he subsequently married three or four years after Alexander's birth.

Badenoch had originally been a Comyn title, but Alexander received the grant of the Badenoch lands from his father on 30 March 1371. With the lordship of Badenoch went the famous Lochindorb Castle, the island stronghold built for Comyn in the 13th century. The Wolf almost immediately started to use this as the base for his terrorising activities. In fact, his sabre (or claymore) rattling had already started there when in August 1370 he had promised the Bishop of Moray, Alexander Burr, protection for his lands and tenants within Badenoch and Strathspey. (Protection rackets did not begin with the Chicago Mafia in the 1920s!)

As King's lieutenant and justiciary north of the Forth he held court at the standing stones in the Rath of Kingussie, and in later days in his castle, Ruthven, in Badenoch. A serious argument between him and the Bishop of Moray occurred there in October 1380. The Bishop, who must have been a brave man for he had the lieutenant decree burnt publicly, denied the Wolf's jurisdiction and appealed direct to the crown. To humiliate a man as powerful, as violent and as self-loving as Alexander Stewart in public was throwing more than caution to the winds. Surprisingly, the Lord of Badenoch did not reply with carnage. He took it quite well though a year later, as if in a huff, he renounced jurisdiction over the Church lands in the district. Undoubtedly he lost some protection money.

He had other quarrels with the Bishop. Leaving his wife for a mistress brought about the biggest rift between them – leading to a greater one. In 1390 he led his men into the town of Forres to raze it to the ground. His men were under orders to burn the church buildings. This shows the man's utter fearlessness – or lack of sanity – when in those days the Church was a global power not to be trifled with. But he was indifferent to its power. In fury at the Bishop's resistance to his plundering and ravaging of the north-east, he led a 'lawless band' into Elgin a month later and destroyed the hospital and the houses of the clergy by setting fire to them. His *coup de grâce* was Elgin Cathedral – thought to be the most beautiful in Scotland – which he also burnt. It was that abomination that earned him his nickname 'the Wolf of Badenoch' and for which he was excommunicated.

There is no record of the number of people he slaughtered on his rampages but it must have been considerable for he was notorious even in that violent age. However, if his career thus far was astonishing in its audacity, the *volte face* that followed was astounding. The Wolf was absolved by the Bishop of St Andrews in the Blackfriars' Monastery at Perth to which he walked barefoot, draped in penitential robes, through gaping crowds. There he confessed his sin publicly to the Bishops of Dunblane, Dunkeld and St Andrews.

What brought about the 'repentance' of such a vicious and callous man is hard to conceive. Almost certainly it was either superstition or political expediency – perhaps he had second thoughts about the Church's power, which, in the 14th century, was absolute. R.B. Cunninghame-Graham, in his forward to the sixth edition of Sir Thomas Dick Lauder's *The Wolfe of Badenoch,* wrote: 'though he harried and plundered Mother Church, he died a saved, good Christian at the heart, when his wild oats were reaped.' Mr Cunninghame-Graham felt this was a sad ending. Not being a lover of penitents, he felt it would have been better for posterity if the Wolf had gone to his grave a wolf, incorrigible and unrepentant.

The Wolf was laid to rest in Dunkeld Cathedral under a now defaced effigy of himself in armour. That he died in absolution is shown by the closed hands on the statue's breast. (His death is often recorded as having happened in 1394. This error was first published by Duncan Stewart in his *History of the Stewarts* in 1734 and was repeated by later writers. However, on 3 May 1398, he was ordered by Robert III to deliver up Spynie Castle to the Bishop of Moray and in 1492 the King wrote to him as Crown Bailie over the Earldom of Athole. The exchequer rolls of Scotland – among other manuscripts – point to his death as being sometime between the end of 1404 or the beginning of 1405.)

Writing of the Wolf's headstone, David Graham Campbell in his *Scotland's Story in Her Monuments* says, 'there is the elaborate armoured figure of Margaret's grandson, the Wolf of Badenoch, at Dunkeld – though no man ever deserved less to have a place of honour in a church . . . The side panels are not, as often, heraldic but of armed men, which is more appropriate as there was nothing chivalrous about the Wolf.'

If mediocrity was a fault it was the only one the Wolf did not have.

The Bestial Beans

Sawney Bean and the Bean family

There is hardly an era in Scottish history that is not
marred by appalling brutality. As we have seen earlier
in this book, the reign of James I was no exception. But
one family, who lived in Galloway during the reigns of
Robert III and James I, must rank as the most heinous
not only of their time but of their country's history.

The head of the family was Sawney Bean who
was born in East Lothian 'about nine miles east of
Edinburgh'. His father worked as a hedger and ditcher
and hoped his son would take up the same employ-
ment. But Sawney, idle and dishonest by nature, had
no intention of following a laborious occupation. While
still in his teens he ran away to the most deserted part of
the country he could find 'taking with him a woman as
viciously inclined as himself'.

They settled in a seaside cave somewhere on the
Galloway coast where they lived for over 25 years.
During that time they had a great number of children
and grandchildren whom they brought up to live as
hermits. None of them ever visited a city, town or a
village in their lives. These strange hermits lived solely
by robbery and those they robbed – man, woman or
child – they murdered.

The people of Galloway grew alarmed by the
frequency with which friends, neighbours and travellers went missing in their county. Many people going
about their personal, lawful businesses disappeared
without trace before the government decided to act by
sending spies in to the area. They too disappeared. The
few who did return had nothing to report; their searches
uncovered nothing.

Public outcry grew to a fever pitch when limbs and
bones were found on beaches after being washed in by
the tides. Word of those murders spread the length and
breadth of Scotland. Several travellers were arrested on
suspicion and hanged. Innkeepers, too, were executed
because those who had disappeared were last seen in
their taverns. Not one of those executed confessed at
the gallows. Every last one maintained his innocence to

the end. Things became so bad that many innkeepers gave up their business for fear of being accused, and inevitably executed. This made life more difficult for travellers.

History has not recorded the exact number of the Bean family other than it 'had grown very large, and every branch of it, as soon as able, assisted in perpetrating their wicked deeds, which they still followed with impunity'. It is hardly surprising that they acted with impunity because they took their victims – or at least their remains – to the cave where they lived. When the tide was in the water reached about a mile inside so that any of the government's armed searchers could have passed the cave's entrance without taking much notice, 'never supposing any human being would reside in such a place of perpetual horror and darkness'.

Besides, the Beans were extremely cunning. They would attack up to six people at once after they had stalked them and made sure escape was impossible. They would place ambushes on every side so that even if their victims managed to escape one group of assailants the large Bean family would have members posted in other positions waiting for them. And they would never attack more than two people on horseback. This shrewd strategy prevented their detection for decades.

But their reign of terror – and their reason for it – was discovered when one intended victim did escape their clutches. The man involved was riding home one evening from a fair with his wife behind him on the same horse. Suddenly, the merciless Beans ambushed. Though the attack was unexpected and frenzied, the man shot a couple of them and defended himself with his sword. Through excellent horsemanship he rode down some Beans with the power of his steed. But at one point, when the horse reared, his wife fell off and was almost instantly butchered. As the husband slashed at the male Beans, the females were on the wife. They slashed her throat and 'fell to sucking her blood as with a great gust, as if it had been wine'. They then ripped open her belly and tore out her entrails. Seeing the fate that awaited him at the hands of these cannibals, the man fought all the harder. Fortunately for him about 30 others returning from the same fair came riding down the road, hastening onwards when they heard the commotion. Realising more travellers approached, Sawney Bean and his clan ran off into the thick wood

towards their den, leaving the man to be the first to fall into their hands and retain his life.

The man, showing the company his wife's mutilated body, told them of what had happened. The astonished and horrified travellers took him to Glasgow where the story was related to the magistrates. They in turn sent couriers to the King reiterating the story. Now the mystery of the Galloway disappearances and the bones on the beaches was solved. A pack of cannibals were roaming the countryside.

About three or four days later, King James set out for the place where the savage attack took place. His company of 400 or so armed men searched all the rocks and thickets for Sawney's clan of cannibals. They were led by the man who had been attacked, and had a 'large number of bloodhounds with them, that no human means be wanting towards putting an entire end to the cruelties'. They searched for some time without finding any clues. When they first passed the Beans' cave they took no notice of it, intending to move on along the beach while the tide was out. Luckily, some bloodhounds ran into the cave.

Instantly they howled and barked and yelped. The King and his attendants returned to see why the hounds were behaving so strangely. They could not imagine how any human beings could be concealed in such an infernally dark place. But the further the hounds went in, the louder they barked and howled, and the searchers realised the animals were reacting to something inexplicable. Eventually they arrived at the furthest possible recess of the cave where the cannibals dwelt.

The King and his men were utterly shocked and appalled at their discovery. 'Legs, arms, thighs, hands, and feet of men, women and children were hung up in rows, like dried beef; a great many limbs laid in pickle, and a great mass of money, both gold and silver, with watches, rings, swords, pistols and a large quantity of cloths, both linen and woollen, and an infinite number of other things which they had taken from those they had murdered, were thrown together in heaps or hung up against the sides of the den.'

The whole Bean clan were seized and pinioned. They consisted of Sawney, his wife, eight sons, six daughters, 18 grandsons and 14 granddaughters – conceived in incest. The King's men took all the human flesh they could find and buried it. They then returned to Edinburgh with their prisoners and their spoils. As word spread that the Beans had been apprehended, crowds flocked to see them as they passed through the country.

When they arrived in Edinburgh they were imprisoned in the tolbooth. The following day they were taken in shackles to the Mercat Cross at Leith where they were executed. They were not given a trial, this being considered needless for such 'professed enemies of mankind'.

The men were tied to stakes. They were dismembered, their hands and legs were cut off and they were left to bleed to death. It took a few hours for them to expire. The wife, daughters and granddaughters were punished by being forced to witness the bloody, torturous execution of their menfolk. Then they were burned to death in three separate fires. Not only did they not show any signs of remorse, but they 'continued cursing and vending the most dreadful imprecations to the very last gasp of life'.

Cruel was the Foe
The Massacre at Glencoe

Few clans have such a bad reputation as the Campbells. Although the chief of the Glenorchy Campbells could travel from the eastern banks of Loch Tay to the coast of Argyll without leaving his own lands, his extensive dominion was gained to the detriment of other clans, mainly MacDonalds, MacGregors, MacLeans and MacDougals. As a result, the Campbells were intensely disliked. They were the first Highland clan to become Protestant and commentators have suggested that they did so for political gain rather than for religious belief. They have been called the Highlands' first politicians.

The event that has most soured their reputation in the eyes of posterity was the so-called 'Massacre of Glencoe'. However, the part they played in this was really no more that that of willing pawns. The blame for the attack on the MacDonalds of Glencoe lies at the door either of Sir John Dalrymple, Master of Stair, or of the King, William of Orange, who signed the Glencoe MacDonalds' 'death warrant'.

William was weary of the troubles in Scotland. He thought that the best way to establish law and order would be to grant an amnesty to the rebel Highland chiefs. There was a condition attached: those chiefs who had not already done so were to acknowledge allegiance by 1 January 1692. On receiving word from the exiled James in France that they could 'do what may be most for their own safety', all the rebel chiefs complied – with the exception of the MacDonald chief, Maclain of Glencoe.

In an attempt to preserve his fast-fading dignity, Maclain put off taking the oath of allegiance until the last possible moment. His procrastination backfired. Fierce blizzards – during an unexpected and particularly bitter winter – delayed him. When he eventually arrived in Fort William, he discovered that he had come to the wrong place and could not find a magistrate to witness his oath. It was 6 January before he could pledge his allegiance and he wept as he asked for his word to be accepted.

Sir John Dalrymple had an antipathy for all Highlanders, and he particularly disliked the MacDonalds, who had a long history of being incorrigible thieves, murderers, rebels – and Catholics to boot. Consequently, the Master of Stair felt if that 'thieving tribe were rooted out and cut off' he would be doing the nation a great service. Maclain's procrastination afforded him an opportunity he could not miss. He wrote at the time, 'I am glad Glencoe did not come within the time prescribed. I hope what's done there may be in earnest.' And when he asked the King whether he could make an example of the clan, he neglected to inform him of Maclain's belated submission. Thinking he was dealing with unrepentant rebels, William gave the order to wipe out Maclain's clan.

They picked the right man to lead the two companies of Campbell soldiers used in the extermination of the Glencoe clan. Captain Robert Campbell of Glenlyon must have felt he had every right to wipe out these MacDonalds. The second time they looted and burnt his glen had completed his financial ruin – begun by drink and gambling – and forced him at the age of 60 into service in the Earl of Argyll's regiment.

At the beginning of February he took his two companies into Glencoe and asked for quarters. It was traditional for Highlanders to offer hospitality to whoever wandered on to their lands, bitter enemies included, and although the MacDonalds may have been severely tempted to turn on the detested Campbells and slay them as they stood, hospitality overcame revenge. The Campbells were wined, dined and housed. It is for betraying that tradition of Highland hospitality that the Campbells have long been loathed in the north. More than the butchery itself, the treachery appalled all who heard of it.

The Campbells stayed in Glencoe for nearly a fortnight till, at midnight on 12 February, when the MacDonalds were asleep, Glenlyon gave the order and his soldiers set to work – if murder can be called work. Maclain, one of the very few MacDonalds still awake, was shot through the head by one of his guests while calling for wine to be brought to them. His dead wife's fingers were bitten off so that a Campbell soldier could get her rings. Thirty-six of his men were slaughtered in their cabins or against their walls outside. The 200 or so who did escape made for the snow-covered mountains. Although many died of exposure it was the snow storm that helped them to escape – that and the incompetence of Glenlyon. He had been ordered to destroy all males under 70 but failed. Perhaps some of the soldiers were reluctant but enough were enthusiastic; the severed hand of a child, for instance, was found later on a dungheap.

By Highland standards what happened that night at Glencoe was not a massacre. The Glencoe men themselves had been involved in bloodier ones – and not on the side of the victims. But this was 'murder under trust'. It was a planned, deliberate, albeit unsuccessful, attempt at genocide, ordered by the government.

The only consolation for the MacDonalds is that the Campbells, with two companies of soldiers armed to the teeth, could not kill a mere 200 of them unarmed. With treachery, surprise and darkness aiding them they butchered less than 40.

Murder Incorporated
Burke and Hare

Scotland has been in the forefront of medicine since the time of the Renaissance and, consequently, at times in her history has harboured a flourishing trade in dead bodies. The law of supply and demand dictates that if surgeons require corpses upon which to practise, there will always be men prepared to provide them with the essential bodies, even if they have to rob graves to do so.

A law of 1505 permitted anatomists the use of 'one condemned man after he be dead' and an act of 1694 allowed them to use the bodies of people who died in the correction house – vagrants, suicides and those publicly executed. But there never seemed enough corpses available.

Due to the demand, body-snatching became a popular occupation and some churches laid huge iron gates over fresh graves to prevent it. The church of St Madoes, in the village of the same name, in Perthshire, still has some of those plates. However, as the body-snatchers (or 'resurrectionists' as they were euphemistically called) could earn more from one body than they could from a month's hard labour, the iron plates were not much of a deterrent.

In the early 1820s a brilliant Edinburgh surgeon named Robert Knox often required corpses. Because he would pay ten pounds for a good one – and no questions asked – he was the resurrectionist's ideal customer.

William Burke stumbled into the business more or less by chance. After leaving his wife in Ireland in 1818, he set off for Edinburgh where he met a fellow Irish exile called William Hare. Hare lived in a hovel called Log's lodging house in Tanner's Close. Although Burke was a neat man who bore a dignified carriage, Hare, an uncouth and coarse man, was said to be worse than an animal, 'the most brutal man ever subjected to my sight'.

Hare had married the landlady of his lodging house and the lodgings helped them in their body business as lodgers frequently died there. Their introduction to the business was when an old man expired without having paid his debt of four pounds for a few weeks' bed and board. Almost without discussion they agreed it fair enough exchange that his corpse should pay for the debt. So they lifted it from its coffin, replacing it with tanner's bark, and sold it to Dr Knox.

Though, unlike other resurrectionists, Burke and Hare did not have to go digging graves on cold, dark nights to make their fortunes, they became too impatient to wait for their lodgers to die. They entered their business seriously by holding a pillow over a sick miller's face. Encouraged that the doctor paid without questions, they then helped a young Englishman who had contracted jaundice to get over it the same way.

They went from bad to worse, always murdering to get their ten pounds. In 1828 when they took the body of an Abigail Simpson to Dr Knox, he remarked on how impressed he was by its freshness. They had met the woman the night before and got her drunk. Ironically, they got too drunk to kill her. When they woke in the morning they got her drunk again and held her mouth and nose until she died.

At one point they came near to being discovered. Burke met two 18-year-old girls in a tavern. One, Mary Paterson, was so beautiful that nobody who saw her could forget her. She was also well-known as a local wanton, making it an act of gross stupidity to attempt her murder. As Burke and Hare's trade depended on obscurity, they must have become either too confident or too greedy because they not only murdered her but they came very near to murdering her friend. It happened after Burke invited them home – home, in fact, to his brother Constantine's house.

It did not take long before Mary became drunk. Try as he might, Burke could not get her friend, Janet Brown, in the same condition. A squabble broke out and she left. After walking the streets for a bit she began to worry about Mary. As soon as she found another friend to back her up she returned with her to Constantine's. It was twenty past ten in the morning and Mary, whom she'd left twenty minutes earlier, was now dead; her body was hidden in the house. Burke had already gone to discuss the deal with Dr Knox.

Constantine invited her in to wait for him. Janet did not know how near she was to death but, to her extreme good fortune, her landlady had heard of where she was and sent a maid to fetch her. Burke missed a double sale.

Burke became bolder still – or greedier. When two officers were arresting a drunk for vagrancy, he said that he knew her and could take her home. Glad to be free of a troublesome customer, they complied and Burke earned another ten pounds for the favour.

One day Burke and Hare met a destitute Irishwoman with her deaf-mute grandson. They found out from the woman that she and her grandson had been roaming the streets for some time in search of friends who had moved to Edinburgh. Feigning pity, they offered her a room. When they took her there they got her drunk and murdered her. At first they were going to turn the boy out on the streets but on second thoughts they decided he could be dangerous, deaf-mute or not. Burke then broke the boy's back over his knee. His body was stuffed into a barrel and taken by horse and cart to Surgeon's Square.

There is no knowing how many people these traders of human flesh murdered during their nine-month partnership. They had become so callous that Hare's wife tried to incite Burke to murder his common-law wife, Helen MacDougal. Apparently she did not like the woman. Burke refused, although the suggestion did not seem to bother him. He was more annoyed at Hare for doing a job without his aid and pocketing the full fee. In fact, he was so incensed that he and MacDougal left their lodgings at Log's. Nevertheless, the partnership continued as it was too lucrative to terminate.

Mrs Hare did get some satisfaction in regard to her dislike of MacDougal: Anne MacDougal, a relative of Helen's, went to see them one day when she was visiting Edinburgh and was smothered to death. The next victim was a charwoman, followed by a prostitute who was in turn followed by her daughter who went to Log's lodgings to look for her.

The murder of Daft Jamie indicates that Dr Knox knew exactly how his suppliers obtained their wares. Daft Jamie was a familiar sight in the city. He was a half-wit, often followed by urchins calling him names. It was easy to lure him into Log's lodgings but, because he did not like alcohol, they could not get him drunk. He fought heroically before Burke and Hare overpowered and then murdered him. But when his body was laid on the dissecting table the students immediately identified him. Knox was emphatic it was not Daft Jamie but, as soon as the boy was reported missing, he dissected the body to remove all evidence.

They were eventually caught, aptly enough on Halloween 1828. They threw a drinking bout in Log's lodgings to celebrate the event. At least that was the impression they wanted to give: the binge was really a front for another murder. And almost immediately after it happened a reveller who heard a cry for help went to fetch a policeman – unsuccessfully. Some of the guests who had managed to remain fairly sober noticed that a Mrs Docherty had disappeared. When they asked where she had gone they were given unclear replies.

One woman became highly suspicious when Burke was furious at her for searching under a bed for her stockings. Realising something was amiss, she waited for the chance to look again. As soon as the murdering duo's attentions were elsewhere, she moved back some straw underneath the bed to uncover the bloodstained and naked corpse of Mrs Docherty.

The woman and her husband said they were going to the police. Burke and Hare threatened them but, seeing that they were not intimidated, they begged them and even offered them an enormous bribe. It must have been tempting to poor folk – especially in those days when abject poverty was the norm. If it was a temptation, they did not succumb. They went to the police and Burke and Hare were arrested. For all the good it did. Hare turned Crown Witness against Burke and MacDougal for his own acquittal. The authorities had to accept the deal as there was no other evidence.

MacDougal was released after a verdict of 'Not Proven', but Burke received the death sentence. As the judge passed sentence, he said to Burke, 'If it is ever customary to preserve skeletons, yours will be preserved, in order that posterity may keep in remembrance your atrocious crimes.' And it has. It can still be seen in the Anatomical Museum of the University of Edinburgh.

Though justice was not truly seen to be done (even Dr Knox could not be charged as the trial only dealt with the Docherty case) there was a kind of poetic justice: Burke's body was publicly dissected. Dr Knox was not given the job; and the outraged Edinburgh public saw to it that his brilliant career came to an abrupt end.

Seven Blythswood Square
Madeleine Smith

Twenty-one-year-old Madeleine Smith, darling of Glasgow Victorian society, the belle of its balls, would not be remembered today but for her affair with a poor clerk from Jersey called Pierre Emile l'Angelier. It made her notorious.

This beautiful young lady, the product of a genteel English boarding school, became famous for a month because of her part in a sordid murder. She hit the Victorian headlines during her trial, which started on 30 June 1837 and ended nine days later.

L'Angelier had seen Madeleine several times in the street and became obsessed with her. He knew he had very little chance of getting to know her as he was a clerk earning a mere ten shillings a week while her father was a very wealthy, highly respected and extremely influential man, an architect by profession. He owned a country house at Rhu on the Clyde and a town house in Glasgow's India Street.

But L'Angelier was determined. One day when she was strolling with her younger sister Bessie in Sauchiehall Street he got a mutual friend, a youth called Robert Baird, to introduce them. As Baird conversed with Madeleine, L'Angelier slipped a note for her to Bessie telling her to pass it on when they got home.

From then on the couple wrote to each other and met for a while in secret; Bessie was the courier of their correspondence. One day Mr Smith discovered the secret and made Madeleine terminate the relationship. So Madeleine wrote to L'Angelier to break it off.

They also used another go-between, an elderly lady called Mary Perry. Being romantically inclined, she encouraged the relationship. Madeleine listened to her and so it carried on. Before long, L'Anglier was being admitted into the India Street house when the rest of the family was asleep. By the spring of 1856 they even dared to meet after dark in her father's country house at Rhu. By then she had become his mistress.

The following winter the Smiths moved to 7 Blythswood Square – not far from Doctor Pritchard's last address. L'Anglier often went there also after the family were asleep and Mary Perry continued to act as their go-between. However, Madeleine began to tire of her lover after a few weeks in the new family home. To make matters worse for L'Anglier, she started seeing another man, William Minnoch, a close friend of her father. Though Minnoch was an older man her father encouraged the courtship. Minnoch had much easier access to her than had L'Anglier for, besides being her father's friend, he was their next-door neighbour.

The couple became engaged and Madeleine wrote to L'Angelier to say she wished to finish the affair and asked that he return her letters. He refused, demanding once more that the affair continue or he would show the letters to her father. She begged his mercy but, seeing he was relentless, continued the affair and wrote him letters as passionately as before. In these she begged him to come to see her, no doubt with the intention of murdering him. Not only did she sit in her room in 7 Blythswood Square considering murder but there she planned it and there she carried it out.

The building still stands, converted into offices some time ago, and people still come from all over the world to see it. Until the first half of the 1980s it was still possible to stand outside the basement bedroom window through which she passed poisoned cocoa to L'Angelier.

Three times within the two months of her writing to terminate the affair, he became extremely ill with internal pains and vomiting. The third attack was fatal. He died in his lodgings on the morning of 23 March 1857.

The sudden death struck his employers and friends as peculiar. The post-mortem showed that he had been poisoned with a large dose of arsenic: 82 grains were found in his stomach alone. Obviously murder was suspected and as Madeleine's letters were found in his rooms and at his work, she was arrested and charged.

Naturally, she denied the murder. However, there was evidence that she had bought arsenic from a local chemist, saying it was for the gardener at their country house and the following evening the poor clerk had had a violent bout of sickness that racked him with pain. It was his second attack; apparently she had poisoned him once before. It was known that she did enquire in some chemists' shops for prussic acid not long before his first attack. Soon after the second, she bought an

ounce of arsenic from another chemist, saying it was to kill rats in her house. When she went back for another ounce she explained it was because it was so effective. However, she told Minnoch that she bought the stuff for her complexion.

Her father took to bed for a while. The family were too ashamed to be seen in public in those days of fierce Victorian prudery and retired to their house at Rhu. Not one of them went to court to comfort her. They despised her for ruining their lives. Their high society days were over; they left Glasgow and went to live near Falkirk. The Burgh Chamberlain there wrote of them: 'They might as well be in the centre of Africa; they visit nobody and nobody visits them.'

Madeleine's last letter to L'Angelier was found in his pocket. It was full of passion and in it she begged him to come and see her. A strange letter for one soon to be married to another – unless she wanted to kill him. But, almost unbelievably, the court's opinion seemed to be in her favour. Perhaps, as one writer suggested, it had a lot to do with class-conscious Victorian values: the Channel Islander was a penniless, working-class upstart who had seduced a young woman of breeding, culture and wealth and had ruined all her future prospects.

His diary, on the orders of two of the three judges, was not considered permissible evidence, though its pages showed he was severely ill each time he had paid his mistress a visit. It was extremely incriminating evidence.

Madeleine sat in the dock a picture of innocence. Although the nation was shocked by the affair, many young men obviously were not. Countless numbers wrote to her proffering marriage. She is said to have been 'ravishing' as she sat in the dock without saying a word. (People charged with murder were not allowed to give evidence at that time.) 'She had fair rosy skin, dark eyes and hair of polished ebony that swept down beside her temples.' It was as if she could bewitch everyone – including the jury. When they acquitted her on a verdict of 'Not Proven' it was received with wild enthusiasm and cheering. Of the jury of 15 only two voted her guilty. It has been said that most of the jury actually believed she *was* guilty.

Though her family went into hiding she did nothing of the sort. A letter she wrote to the matron of Edinburgh prison four days after the trial ended showed she cared little for public opinion – in the age when most were slaves to it. She told the matron that she was 'slightly piqued' at the attitude towards her in the west of Scotland and that it 'may' be necessary for her to go away for a few months.

She moved to Plymouth where she met and married a young artist. He travelled to India not long after and did not return. He said he 'didn't like the look in her eye'. Perhaps he realised she *was* a murderess. But it did not appear to bother her. Under her new name, she became well known in Bloomsbury circles. She championed the Bohemians and shocked Victorian prudes by being the first to do away with long table-cloths, revealing the bare legs of tables – outrageous behaviour in the eyes of the people of that era.

She emigrated to the USA in 1916 where she married again though an elderly woman. She died in New York twelve years later at the age of 95.

Murderer's Justice
Thomas 'Bonnie' Scobie

'Bonnie Scobie' was the somewhat sarcastic appellation Angus folk gave to a dirty, ugly tramp called
Thomas Scobie. He was originally from Dunfermline
but the 36-year-old down-and-out Fifer spent much of
his adulthood wandering around Angus and Forfarshire.
His claim to fame is that he was a murderer.

It happened on the morning of 24 September 1872,
when some washing had been stolen from the line of
a family in Kilgennie. George Spalding, head of the
family, was told of the theft by his sister when he arrived
home. Some of his neighbours told him that a tramp
had been in the area and was acting suspiciously, so
he set off to look for the culprit.

Eventually he found Scobie. As he seemed the likeliest
candidate Spalding called upon him to own up. After
a heated argument Scobie was forced to deliver the
clothes from where he had stashed them. Even then he
still protested his innocence and blamed the theft on a
friend. But Spalding was not convinced and, making
a citizen's arrest, ordered him to accompany him to
Monifieth Police Station.

At one point Scobie tried to escape. Spalding, being
a gamekeeper, had a dog with him and he set it after
the tramp. It caught him and pinned him to the ground.
Later, as they approached Monifieth, the men argued
violently. Scobie's attitude infuriated the gamekeeper
so much that he became extremely abusive. Scobie
reacted by trying to strangle him. Spalding passed out
and as he fell his head struck a boulder. Or so goes the
story passed down to us, though no-one can say what
exactly occurred during the encounter. But Spalding's
head was badly smashed when his body was discovered the following day.

He died around 4 p.m. – the same day he fought
with Scobie. His family were not particularly concerned when he did not return that evening: his work
often took him away overnight. It was not till around
eight thirty the following morning – well past his usual
breakfast-time when his dog returned home alone. The

Spaldings started to worry because this had never happened before.

They contacted the Dundee police. The descriptions they gave of the tramp pointed to Scobie: his appearance was so repulsive it could only have been 'Bonnie Scobie'. As he had previous convictions he was well known to the police. When he was duly arrested, his trousers showed they had been ripped by what the police said were 'like a dog's teeth' and his shirt was bloodstained. Friends he had visited in Dundee's Overgate, on the night of the murder, told the police his face had been badly scratched and covered in blood.

Because he denied the murder he was put to a test, then a feature of Scots' law. He was taken into a room where the murdered body was lying and made to look at it. Then the police asked, 'Did you ever see that man before? Did you murder him?' This was good psychology for its time. Those were the days when most people still had a belief in Divine retribution. Those like Scobie, who didn't believe it in the Christian sense, certainly did in a superstitious way. Normally, making a murderer stand in front of the body he robbed of life, would cause him to crack and admit his guilt. But Scobie was not normal! He was willing to swear on the corpse – or anything else if he had to – that he was innocent. He looked at it and said, 'Naw, naw. I'm bad and bad enough as the polis ken. But I'm no' a murderer.'

A jury at the Dundee Circuit Court begged to differ. They found him guilty by 14 votes to one at a trial held the following April. And though they recommended mercy, Lord Deas, the judge, issued the following sentence:

In respect of the said verdict of Assize against the panel, Lord Deas and Lord Jerviswood discern and adjudge the said Thomas Scobie, panel, to be carried from the bar back to the prison of Dundee, therein to be detained, and fed on bread and water only, until Tuesday, the 29th day of April next to come, and upon that day, betwixt the hours of eight and ten o' clock forenoon, within the walls of the said prison, to be hanged by the neck upon a gibbet by the hands of the common executioner, until he be dead, and ordain the said body thereafter to be buried within the walls of the said prison, which is pronounced for doom.

Fortunately for Scobie, the judge made a blunder. When writing out the sentence Lord Deas forgot it was already the month of April. There would not be a 'Tuesday, the 29th day of *April next to come*' for another six years! It was obvious enough what the judge meant, but the letter of the law had to be adhered to.

Scobie had another stroke of luck. The public in general sympathised with him, believing he had been provoked beyond reason and a petition bearing 4300 signatures was sent to the Home Secretary.

What with Lord Deas' blunder it seemed best to heed the petition. The government granted a reprieve and the sentence was changed. Scobie was 'to be detained during her Majesty's pleasure.'

He was released from prison in 1897. He returned to his home town, Dunfermline, where he died soon after.

Matricide, Uxoricide and Suicide
John Merrett

John Donald Merrett, though a brilliant scholar, was a
work-shy, self-indulgent, unfeeling waster. When his
mother – a reasonably well-off widow – took him to
Edinburgh in 1926, she did so to keep an eye on him
while he was at university. She knew that if he were to
go to a residential university he would get up to no good
away from her strong influence. She was well aware of
her son's shortcomings. But perhaps they had a lot to
do with the fact that he had been spoiled: as a teenager
he received ten shillings pocket money – when skilled
tradesmen were earning under three pounds a week
and labourers considerably less.

Merrett led a double life almost from the day they
settled in the city. Instead of attending lectures, as
his mother thought he was doing, he wandered the
streets in search of whatever pleasures came his way.
In the evenings he would sneak off to the Dunedin
Palais where he struck up a relationship with one of
the dancing instructors. He ended up squandering all
of his money on her.

Even ten shillings a week was not enough for this
teenager, especially as he was wining, dining and even
buying jewellery for his instructress. He bought two
motorbikes – one with a sidecar; the money had to
come from somewhere so he stole it from his mother.

On 17 March, only a couple of months after they had
arrived in the capital, Merrett committed his first murder. His victim died 14 days after he shot her, spending
most of the time unconscious in hospital.

The morning the shooting took place Mrs Merrett sat
writing at her bureau as her son sat at the opposite side
of the room quietly reading a book. The scene was
quite peaceful. At least that was how it looked when
Mrs Sutherland, the daily help, let herself into their flat
at 31 Buckingham Terrace. After glancing in at them
Mrs Sutherland walked into the kitchen to carry on
with her duties. She was not in there long when she
decided to light a fire and as she was putting flame to
paper, she heard a bang. It was followed by a scream

and then a dull thud. Moments later Merrett appeared at the kitchen door saying, 'Rita, my mother has shot herself.'

When she went back with him to the sitting-room she found Mrs Merrett lying unconscious on the floor, blood gushing from her ear. The pistol was on the bureau. They called for an ambulance and Mrs Merrett was taken to the Royal Infirmary. As she was 'a prisoner charged with attempted suicide', she was put in a ward with barred windows and locked door and no-one – staff or visitors – was allowed to tell her what had happened.

Mrs Merrett did manage to give her story to one doctor before she died: 'I was sitting down writing letters and my son Donald was standing beside me. I said "Go away, Donald, and don't annoy me" and the next I heard was some kind of explosion. And I don't remember any more.'

The doctor was worried by this statement and called the police. The Inspector who dealt with the case was convinced it was a suicide for three reasons. Merrett himself agreed partly with what his mother said. He even volunteered that she had told him to go away. As he did not know that the Inspector already knew this, it must have made him less suspect. He said that as he was going he heard a shot and turned to see his mother falling as a revolver fell to the floor.

Another thing that made him less suspect was that he calmly admitted that the revolver was his and that he loaded it to go shooting rabbits on the Braid Hills – hardly the kind of thing a murderer would really admit to if the gun were his. But, he explained, when his mother saw him with it she confiscated it and put it in a drawer and he had not seen it from that day till her attempt at suicide. His total composure was convincing. The Inspector must have attributed it to innocence rather than callousness – and understandably because something else seemed to point to suicide: the Inspector noticed two letters on Mrs Merrett's bureau; they were from her bank manager and were telling her that her account was overdrawn.

Mrs Sutherland's story – or stories – also helped the young murderer. Her final version was that when she heard a bang from the kitchen she ran to the sitting-room to see Mrs Merrett falling off a chair and a gun falling from her hand. Perhaps Merrett had got her to say this, because it was certainly not the truth. When she entered the room the pistol was on the bureau – according to her first statement.

Mrs Merrett's sister and her husband stayed at Buckingham Terrace to look after Merrett while he continued his studies. Of course, he did not continue them, but carried on as he had before until he was expelled for absenteeism.

Just when John Donald Merrett thought the case was over and forgotten, he was arrested and charged with the murder of his mother and with forging her signature on cheques that he later cashed. The trial started in February 1927. It was easy to prove that he had been stealing from his mother by cashing cheques in her name, but the murder charge was another matter. Because Mrs Sutherland had changed her story so often, her testimony was unreliable and as she was the key witness this made it difficult for the police to make the charge stick. On the charge of murder he was found 'Not Proven', but the jury voted unanimously that he was guilty of theft by the forging of cheques. The 17-year-old Merrett was sent to prison for a year.

When he left prison he went to live with a friend of his mother's in Hastings, a lady called Mrs Bonnar. Merrett repaid her for her kindness and generosity by seducing her teenage daughter Vera and eloping with her to Scotland. They married there as she was old enough to do so under Scots' law. Having changed his name to Chesney, he took her to Edinburgh. His own name would have aroused memories there.

They travelled throughout their honeymoon, never staying very long in one place. Wherever they went Merrett paid the bills with 'bounced' cheques. He was arrested in Newcastle and sentenced to six months' imprisonment. When he was released from Durham prison he carried on life as before, living as a wealthy layabout. He still had an income from his mother's estate, which he squandered, and when he reached the age of 21 he inherited fifty thousand pounds of his grandfather's fortune. With it he bought a large house complete with six servants, a boat and a small aeroplane. He installed his wife and mother-in-law in the house and, instead of settling down to a respectable life as he could now easily do, he went into the smuggling business.

During the Second World War he served as a trainee

officer in the Royal Navy. Even there he was nicknamed 'Crasher' because of his reckless lifestyle. After the war he was imprisoned for stealing a car from the Navy. At the time, the early post-war era, he was a successful black-market operator in Germany where he became 'addicted to drink, women and easy money'. Soon after he had made a name for himself in the black market he was imprisoned in England for smuggling women's stockings.

In 1954 he decided to murder his wife. Some years earlier, on the advice of a trustee who was in charge of his maternal estate, he had made an eight thousand pounds settlement on her. But he now wanted it back. While in Germany he set about planning Vera's death – aided by the latest of a long string of mistresses. He thought he would get into England easily on his forged passport, murder his wife and return secretly to Europe. The perfect murder plan, but the best laid schemes . . .

He got into the country easily enough. But when he drowned his wife in the bath at their Ealing house (run as an old folks' home by Vera and Mrs Bonnar), his mother-in-law surprised him. After she put up a ferocious struggle he strangled her with her own stockings. When other residents found the bathroom locked, and getting no answer, they called the police. They broke down the door to find Vera's body in the bath. Immediately they searched for her mother. Her body was found in an unused storeroom hidden behind a large pile of lumber.

Soon the police had Mrs Chesney's estranged husband, Ronald, high on their enquiries list. By then he was back in Germany. But it was not long before he was the chief suspect – in fact, the only suspect.

One day, in the city of Cologne, he read in the papers that a full-scale murder hunt was on for him. He knew he could not escape the inevitable for much longer so he concluded it in his own inimitable way. He walked into a wooded park in the city and, as easily as he murdered his own mother, wife and mother-in-law, he put a pistol barrel into his mouth, pulled the trigger and killed himself.